THE CHRISTOPHER PARKENING GUITAR METHOD, VOL. 1

THE ART AND TECHNIQUE OF THE CLASSICAL GUITAR

In Collaboration with Jack Marshall and David Brandon

ISBN 978-0-7935-8520-5

HAL•LEONARD®
CORPORATION

7777 W. BLUEMOUND RD. P.O. BOX 13819 MILWAUKEE, WI 53213

Visit Hal Leonard Online at
www.halleonard.com

Dedication

*To my wife Theresa,
my father, mother and sister,
for their untiring, loving guidance
and devotion to my music.*

Acknowledgments

It was in Chicago in 1969 that James Sherry, the highly respected importer of fine guitars, first implanted in my mind the suggestion that I should write a method book. I was staggered by the thought of the enormous amount of time involved and, therefore, politely declined. Mr. Sherry persisted, meeting with me and urging the project by telephone. There had been, he said, few new methods published in this century and none by a concert classical guitarist. It would fill a genuine longstanding need. His unremitting enthusiasm fired my own excitement for the idea and his generous offer to publish the original volume himself supplied the means. It is therefore to my friend James Sherry that I owe great thanks for the initial impetus for *The Christopher Parkening Method*.

I also owe an inexpressible debt of thanks to my gifted cousin Jack Marshall (1921–1973) who was a wise and staunch friend to me from the beginning of my own guitar studies—and never more so than during the writing of this method. I had his invaluable counsel and assistance throughout and the very great benefit of his gifts as a composer, when a beautiful duet or a melodic short study was needed to facilitate the practicing of new techniques I wished to introduce to the student. I thank Chris Amelotte, whose advice and knowledgeable teaching experience were helpful aids in the writing of this method. My deep appreciation also goes to David Brandon, who oversaw the revision of this book, and who added numerous new original studies and pieces.

My gratitude goes to Marvin Schwartz for his valued aid as art consultant, to my editorial consultant Rory Guy, to my art production consultant Mike Hogan, and to the deservedly famous photographer Ken Veeder, who took the many special photographs needed to illustrate the method.

I thank guitar historian Ron Purcell and luthier Tom Beltran for their insightful comments on the Appendix of this book.

I would also like to thank Scott Bach, Pat and Shirley Russ, and Jim Fagen for their assistance in textual changes and proofreading. I am also indebted to all the many students who have inspired revisions through the years.

Typesetting and music layout were handled by David Brandon using *Finale* and *WordPerfect*. I would like to thank the fine staff at Hal Leonard Corporation for their production assistance and overall support.

Contents

Foreword

I first became interested in the guitar in 1959 through the playing of my cousin, Jack Marshall (1921–1973), with whom I wrote the first edition of this book. At the time, Jack was the staff guitarist with MGM Studios. I loved the way he played and wanted to learn to play the guitar. I was eleven and had never played an instrument before.

Jack told me I should start with the classical guitar. Through it, he said, I would learn correctly the basic fundamentals of guitar playing, and after studying the classical style, I would be able to play any style of guitar with greater ease. Jack also recommended that I listen to the recordings of Andrés Segovia who was, he said, the world's greatest guitarist. My father presented me with my first Segovia album. After hearing it, I made the decision to study classical guitar.

The local music store where we purchased a guitar recommended that I study with a Spanish family of classical guitarists who had just settled in Los Angeles. They were the Romeros. In my early training with them, I became still more intrigued with the enchanting sound of the guitar. After a few months, I was able to play some very beautiful little pieces, experiencing the deep enjoyment of playing for my friends and playing solo just for myself.

I developed technique by playing pieces which involved technical exercises. This method encouraged me to practice by making practice enjoyable. Of course, I also played exercises which concentrated on specific techniques that needed developing, but for the most part I learned the guitar by playing pieces I loved and trying to perfect them. This method seems to me by far the best; it is the method I've used since I began to teach, and it is the principle I've applied to this book. Whenever possible, we have selected pieces which incorporate the new musical concepts or techniques the student is to learn. When this has not been possible—in instances where no appropriate pieces seemed to exist—we have used new studies composed by Jack Marshall and David Brandon.

To return briefly to my own early progress, the Romeros began to concertize extensively, and I had to continue on my own. This mastery of the guitar without a teacher became an enormous challenge, and I worked very hard. I found that it was necessary to experiment, sometimes even to risk taking a step backward in order to make the next step forward possible. However, it was tremendously satisfying to try, day by day, to accomplish something and, little by little, to analyze and solve the problems that arose. Throughout this period, I relied heavily on the encouragement and guidance of an unfailing friend who also loves music, my father Duke Parkening.

In 1964, it was announced that Segovia would give his first United States master class at the University of California at Berkeley. My audition tape was sent to Segovia, who gave me a scholarship. Segovia's teaching was invaluable to me. The time I spent learning from him was one of the greatest experiences of my life.

Following the master class, I had several further opportunities to study with Maestro Segovia. In 1968 he extended to me the very great privilege of an invitation to participate as one of the judges in the International Guitar Competition held in Spain. That year marked the beginning of my career as a professional classical guitarist: I founded the guitar department at the University of Southern California where I taught as a full-time professor. Soon after, I signed with Columbia Artists Management, Inc. for a tour of over seventy concerts the first season. Since then I have concertized extensively throughout North America, Europe, and Asia under the auspices of IMG and have released many recordings for EMI/Angel and Sony Classical.

For me, the guitar was an early love that has deepened, year by year, into a profound commitment and a very fulfilling means of expression. I hope this story will encourage you who feel a similar love for the guitar.

This book is designed to present you with a logical and systematic method for gradual and technical development toward the eventual mastery of this great and noble instrument. It is not intended solely for the guitarist who aspires to be a concert performer. It is also for the person unknowledgeable in music who wishes to learn the correct fundamentals, with enjoyment during the learning process, and regardless of age.

Volume One deals with notes covering the first five frets. It presents information in the important fundamentals of guitar playing—much of which has never been presented before. It is arranged concisely and systematically so that you can develop into the kind of guitarist you wish to become, without having to unlearn many hours or years of incorrect practice and study. Volume Two of this method covers notes on the remainder of the fingerboard and includes more advanced work on technique and interpretation.

The guitar is one of the most beautiful, sensitive and poetic instruments in all the world. I will be grateful if I can pass along the knowledge of this instrument to those who love it.

The Guitar

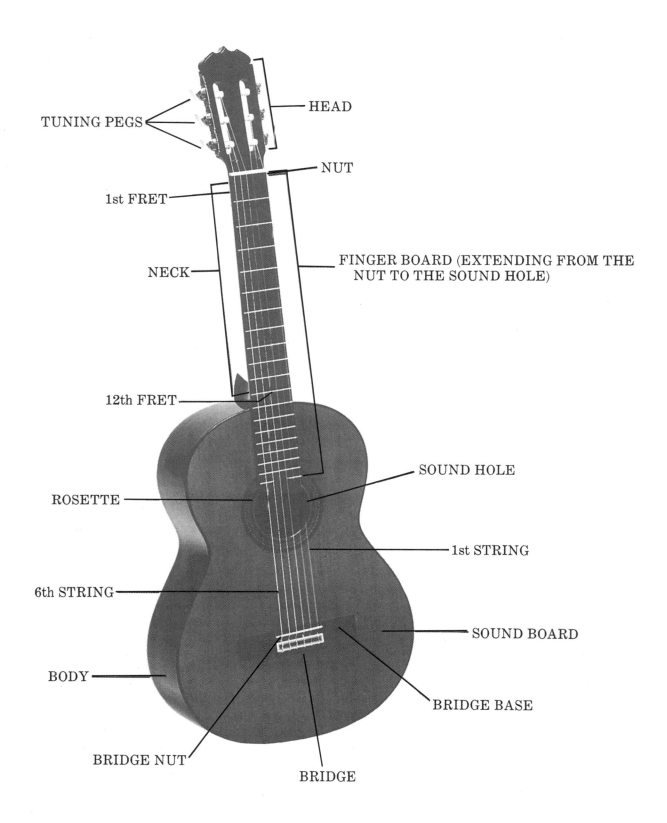

TUNING PEGS

HEAD

NUT

1st FRET

NECK

FINGER BOARD (EXTENDING FROM THE NUT TO THE SOUND HOLE)

12th FRET

ROSETTE

SOUND HOLE

1st STRING

6th STRING

SOUND BOARD

BODY

BRIDGE BASE

BRIDGE NUT

BRIDGE

Author's Note: If you have not yet purchased a guitar, please refer to p. 100 for information on the selection of an instrument. For left-handed players, see note on p. 101.

Parts of the Guitar

TUNING PEGS
Used to tune strings.

STRINGS
The guitar has six strings made of nylon. The strings are numbered ① through ⑥. The 1st string ① has the highest pitch. The higher 1st, 2nd and 3rd are plain, and the lower 4th, 5th and 6th are wound with wire.

NUT
Notched for each string.

FRETS
Raised metallic strips on the fingerboard.

FINGERBOARD
Placed over the neck, spanning from the nut to the edge of the sound hole.

ROSETTE
Decorative inlay around the sound hole.

BRIDGE
Strings are attached here and pass over the bridge nut (saddle).

A guitar maker in Spain.

Holding the Guitar

Use a straight back, armless chair and a footstool from 4 to 6 inches high placed under the left foot.

Sit on the edge of the chair leaning forward into the guitar.

Fig. 1 Sitting position (men).

Fig. 3 Alternate sitting position (women).

Fig. 2 Sitting position (women).

Fig. 4 The sitting position for young people is the same.

Fig. 5

Secure the instrument at four points:

1) Against the body.
2) Inside the forearm on the highest point of the curve of the guitar.
3) Inside the right thigh.
4) Resting on the left leg in the natural curve of the guitar.

The neck of the guitar should be at an approximate 35° angle.

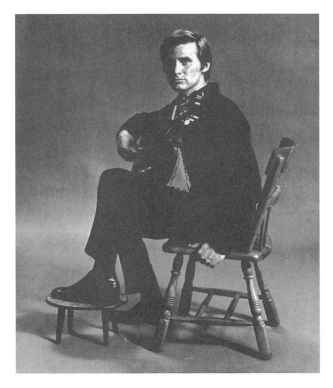

Fig. 7

Notice the space between the back of the guitar and the body of the player, which allows the back of the instrument to vibrate freely for the maximum projection of sound.

Fig. 6 Notice the guitar is not held in a vertical position.

Fig. 8 Notice that the neck of the guitar slants back toward the left shoulder.

Strive to achieve a balance between security, relaxation, and the ability to produce a good sound.

Tuning the Guitar

The first step in tuning the guitar can be accomplished by one of three methods:

1. The Piano

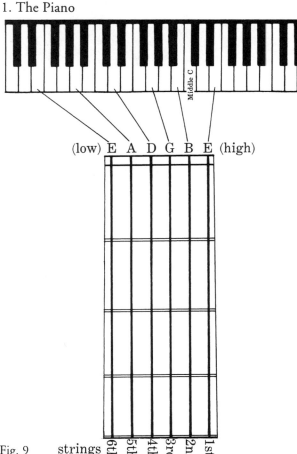

Fig. 9   strings

Tune the guitar strings to match the piano notes as shown above.

2. The Tuner

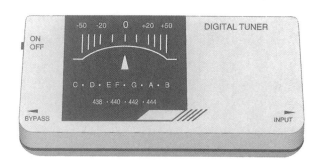

Fig. 10

The battery-operated tuner will register the pitch of each note and indicate whether it should be raised or lowered. These devices are reasonably accurate and are a good investment for students who need help in training their ear.

3. The Tuning Fork

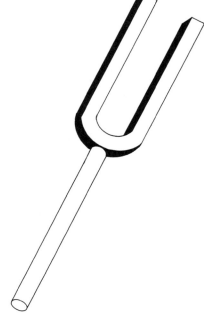

Fig. 11

Using a tuning fork is the most accurate method of determining pitch, although it is more difficult than a tuner. Most tuning forks produce the note "A" (440 vibrations per second). This pitch corresponds to the note found on the 1st or highest sounding string when depressed at the 5th fret.

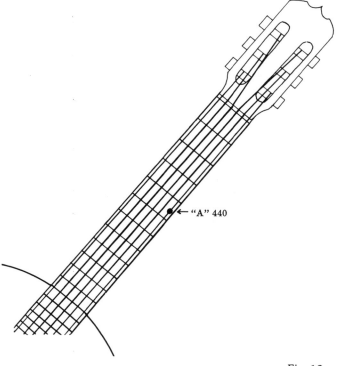

Fig. 12

Note: A pitch pipe is not generally recommended for tuning the guitar. It is not as accurate as the methods mentioned above.

Tuning the guitar (cont.)

It is important that the strings of the guitar be tuned in correct relation to one another or, in other words, the guitar must be tuned to itself (called *relative tuning*). To first obtain the pitch from the tuning fork, hit the fork on your knee to start the vibration. Then place the bottom of the tuning fork on the guitar to amplify the sound. Pluck the open **5th** string and match that note with the tuning fork. Then proceed to tune the guitar to itself, as follows:

Depress the **6th** string at the fifth fret, as shown. Adjust or tune the **6th** string depressed at the fifth fret until it sounds the same (in unison) as the **5th** string open.

Depress the **5th** string at the fifth fret and tune the **4th** open string in unison with the **5th** string depressed at the fifth fret.

Depress the **4th** string at the fifth fret and tune the **3rd** open string in unison with the **4th** string depressed at the fifth fret.

Depress the **3rd** string at the *fourth* fret and tune the **2nd** open string in unison with the **3rd** string depressed at the fourth fret.

Depress the **2nd** string at the fifth fret and tune the **1st** open string in unison with the **2nd** string depressed at the fifth fret.

When you have completed the above, it is advisable to repeat the whole procedure to further refine the intonation.

New strings will require repeated tuning until they become seasoned.

The guitar is a fretted instrument with many variable factors. Tuning it solely to the piano, tuner, or tuning fork is usually insufficient. Relative tuning is an essential procedure for more accurate intonation. As you become more proficient on the guitar, you will be taught still other methods of further refining the tuning.

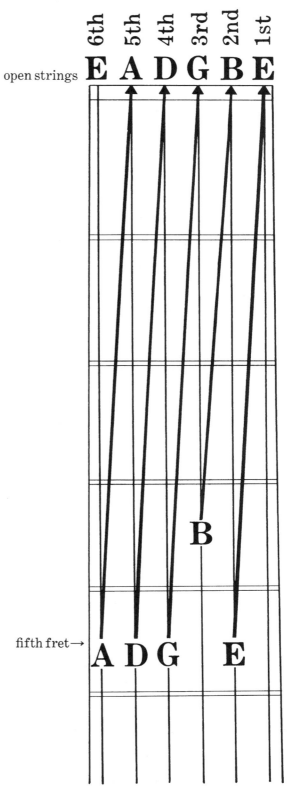

Fig. 13

The Right Hand

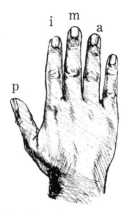

Fig. 14

In guitar music, the thumb is designated by the small letter *p*, the index finger *i*, the middle finger *m*, and the ring finger *a*. The little finger is used only for rasgueados (strums).

The initials designating the right-hand fingers come from the Spanish words.

(p) for *pulgar* or thumb.
(i) for *indice* or index finger.
(m) for *media* or middle finger.
(a) for *anular* or ring finger.

Fig. 15 The right hand is placed toward the lower end of the sound hole.

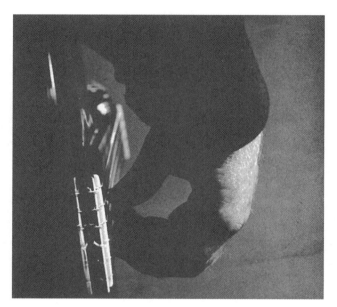

Fig. 17 From the right.

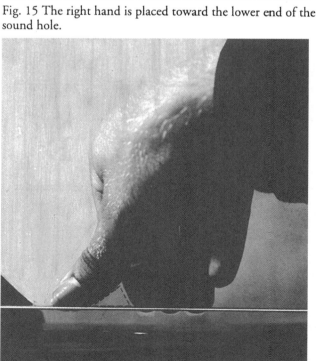

Fig. 16 Player's view. Notice the space between the thumb and the index finger.

Fig. 18 From the left. The hand and forearm should be positioned so that they form a natural arch at the wrist.

There are exceptions to the general rule of right hand placement. Movement of the right hand toward the bridge produces a thinner, more brittle tone which is sometimes desirable. Movement toward the fingerboard produces a rounder, more delicate tone. *Above*: the young Segovia obtains a softer, sweeter tone by placing his right hand directly over the sound hole.

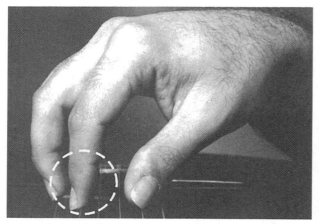

Preparation (index finger) rest stroke.

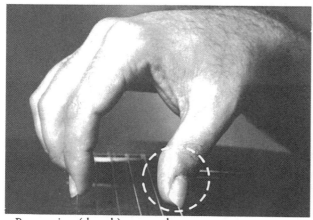

Completion (index finger) rest stroke.

Preparation (thumb) rest stroke.

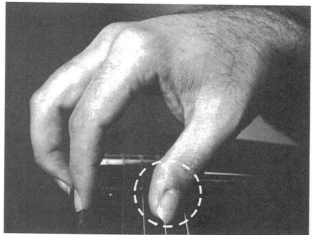

Completion (thumb) rest stroke.

Two Ways of Striking A String

There are two ways to strike a string: the rest stroke (*apoyando* in Spanish) and the free stroke (*tirando*).

The Rest Stroke

When the right-hand fingers or thumb strike a string and are brought to rest against the adjacent string, it is called the rest stroke.

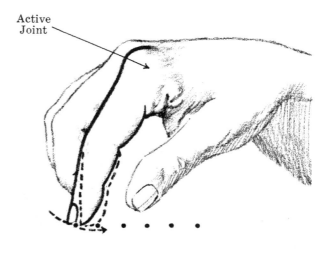

Fig. 19 Rest stroke with a finger.

The fingers are held in an almost straight position except for the *m* finger which, being the longest, bends slightly at the first joint.

The thumb strikes the string in a forward and downward movement coming to rest against the adjacent string. The thumb is only occasionally played rest stroke.

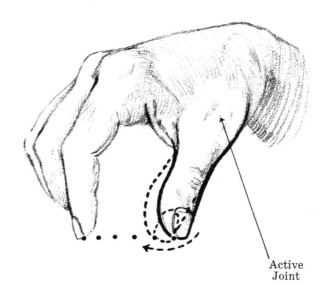

Fig. 20 Rest stroke with the thumb.

The Free Stroke

When the right-hand fingers or thumb strike a string and are lifted slightly to avoid hitting the adjacent string, it is called a free stroke.

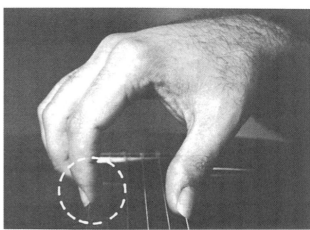

Preparation (index finger) free stroke.

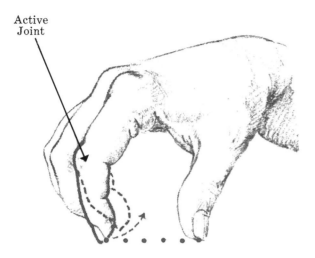

Fig. 21 Free stroke with a finger.

The fingers hang together relaxed and are usually arched, and remain so throughout the stroke. In both the free stroke and rest stroke, the finger motion starts from the knuckles. The fingers should "follow through" in the motion toward the palm.

The thumb strikes the string in a forward and slightly outward movement to avoid hitting the adjacent string. The thumb is most often played free stroke.

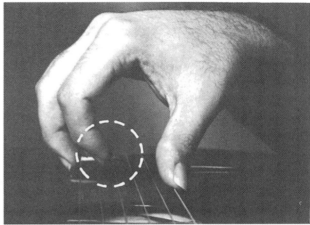

Completion (index finger) free stroke.

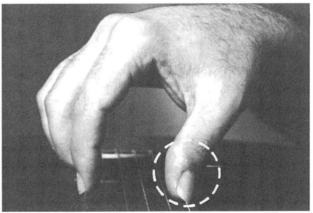

Preparation (thumb) free stroke.

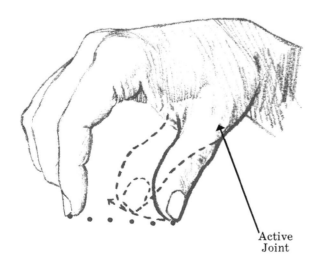

Fig. 22 Free stroke with the thumb.

The rest stroke is used for scale passages or notes of emphasis, as it is louder than free stroke. Otherwise, the free stroke is more often used.

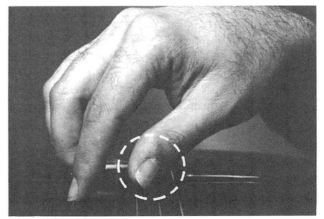

17 Completion (thumb) free stroke.

Fundamentals of Music Notation

1. **Staff:** Musical notes are written on the *staff*, which consists of 5 *lines* and 4 *spaces*:

2. **Clef:** At the beginning of each line of music, there is a *clef sign*. In guitar music, the *treble* (or G) clef sign is used.

3. **Notes:** A note may have the following parts:

Stem — ♪ — Flag
Head — ●

4. **Lines:** The notes on each *line* are named:

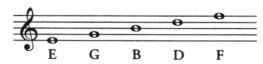

E   G   B   D   F

(The traditional way of remembering the names of the notes on the lines is the use of the phrase, "Every Good Boy Does Fine.")

5. **Spaces:** The notes in each *space* are named:

F   A   C   E

(And, of course, these spell the word "face.")

6. **Ledger Lines:** Notes above or below the staff are shown by additional lines called *ledger lines.*
These are the notes covered in this book above and below the staff:

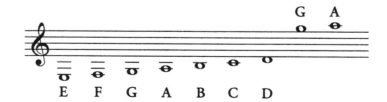

E   F   G   A   B   C   D

7. **Octaves:** The musical alphabet uses the first seven letters of the regular alphabet, starting with A, going to G, then repeating.
     A B C D E F G – A B C D E F G (and continuing to repeat). The distance from one letter to the next letter of the same name is called an *octave* (8 notes).
    Each musical note represents a pitch which can be played in one or more locations on the neck of the guitar. These notes will be learned systematically as you proceed through the book.

Fundamentals of Music Notation (cont.)

8. Measures: The staff is divided into *measures* by *bar lines*. At the end of a piece there is a *double bar line*.

9. Repeat Signs: A dotted double bar line is called a *repeat sign*. It indicates that the preceding measure or measures should be repeated. When you arrive at a repeat sign, return to the facing repeat sign (Ex. A). If there is no facing repeat sign, return to the beginning of the piece (Ex. B).

Ex. B) Repeat from the beginning   **Ex. A) Repeat these four measures**

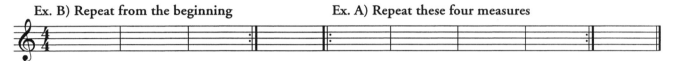

10. Note Values: Music consists of a steady beat, or pulse, and gets its rhythm from notes of different time values. In addition to the note on the staff defining pitch, the type of note indicates its duration. Here is a chart of the most common types of notes and their relative time values:

Comparative Note Values

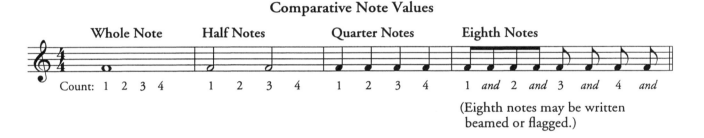

(Eighth notes may be written beamed or flagged.)

11. Time Signature: In the preceding example, you will notice a set of numbers following the clef sign. This is called a time signature. The top number shows the number of counts or beats in one measure. The bottom number shows the type of note which gets one count.

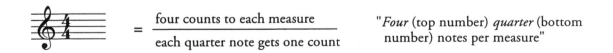

$$\frac{\text{four counts to each measure}}{\text{each quarter note gets one count}}$$

"*Four* (top number) *quarter* (bottom number) notes per measure"

Note: 4/4 time as shown above is sometimes called *common time*, written as:

12. Dot: A dot placed after a note increases the value of the note by half its original duration.

$\sf d \cdot = d + d$ (three counts)

19

Practicing

Correct practicing is the most important habit to develop in becoming a fine guitarist. Without correct practice it is impossible to play the guitar well. For serious study, I recommend that the beginning guitarist practice from one to three hours a day. This practice should be away from distractions, in order to afford maximum concentration. The rate of progress the student makes increases proportionately with the amount of correct practice. It is my understanding that Andrés Segovia practiced four to five hours each day until his death at age 94. Decide how much time you are able to give the instrument each day, and try to accomplish something at each practice session. Always keep in mind that it is better to play one piece well than many pieces poorly.

Before each practice session, be certain of the following:

- That you are seated in the proper position (p. 10).

- That your right and left hands are held in the correct position (p. 14 and p. 26).

- That your guitar is properly tuned (p. 12).

- That you know the purpose of the study, and set for yourself a goal. The goal at first should be to play each study or piece without mistakes, starting at a very slow speed (or tempo) and working up to a faster speed. Increase the tempo as you are able proficiently to do so. A metronome (a device used to beat time) is very helpful; it is, in fact, an indispensable tool for practicing. Select a comfortable, slower tempo on the metronome and play the study in strict rhythm with it. If the study cannot be played without stopping or making mistakes, slow the tempo down and work up to the faster speeds. Ordinarily, you should not increase your tempo more than one metronome setting at a time. Practice the difficult passages separately.

- Do not play too softly. Practice playing with a strong, even sound while striving for full, round tones.

- Cultivate, from the beginning, a technique based upon relaxation. The tension required to play should be confined to the hands, with the rest of the body remaining relaxed.

Rhythm Studies

In the following studies, play the 1st string open (high E) with your right-hand index finger. You may also substitute the open 6th string (low E) played with the thumb. Count aloud or silently. Play slowly enough to keep an even tempo.

Sergovia as Maestro

Notes on the Open Bass Strings

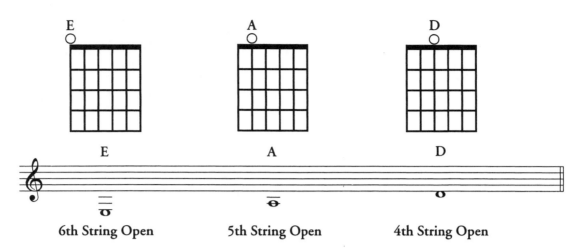

6th String Open   5th String Open   4th String Open

When playing bass notes alone with the thumb, set your *ami* (see p. 14) fingers on strings 1–3 respectively for more security. Play free stroke with the thumb.

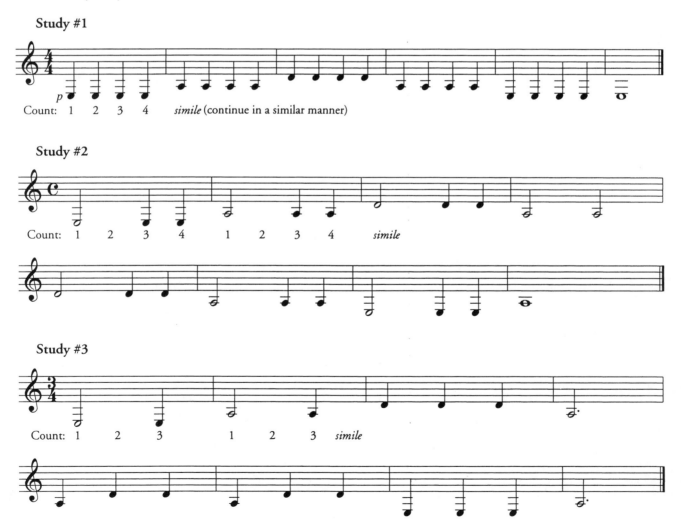

Study #1

Count: 1 2 3 4   *simile* (continue in a similar manner)

Study #2

Count: 1 2 3 4 1 2 3 4   *simile*

Study #3

Count: 1 2 3 1 2 3   *simile*

Open Bass Strings (cont.)

DUETS are used in this method, where suitable, for the purpose of making a study more interesting and enjoyable to play. For the easier duets, the student may invite another beginner to practice with him, with both alternating parts. For the duets with harmonies requiring a more advanced technique, the teacher or a more advanced student may be called upon to play the harder part. In these student–teacher duets, the student part is in the upper line.

DUET ONE

*This sign ⌢ is called a fermata. The note under it should be sustained or held longer than its designated value.

DUET TWO

23

Notes on the Open Treble Strings

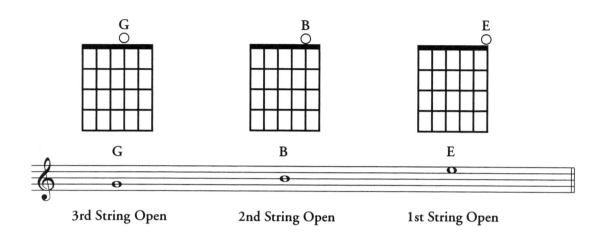

3rd String Open   2nd String Open   1st String Open

On the following exercises, set your thumb lightly on the 6th string for right-hand security. Play free stroke.

Study #4

*Repeat from the beginning.

Study #5 Practice slowly and evenly, graduating to faster speeds.

Count: 1 *and* 2 *and* 3 *and* 4 *and* *simile*

Study #6

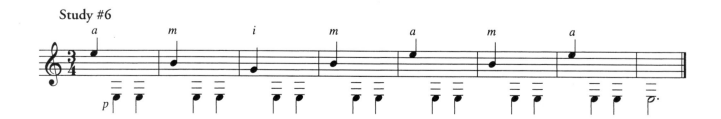

Study #7

Study #8

For more efficiency when playing repeated notes on the same string, alternate the *i* and *m* fingers. Set the thumb lightly on the 6th string for more support. Try rest stroke and free stroke.

Study #9

DUET THREE

25

The Left Hand

Here are the names of the left-hand fingers:

The numbers are used in guitar music to denote specific left-hand fingerings.

1 – index finger

2 – middle finger

3 – ring finger

4 – little finger

0 – open string

The thumb is not used to depress a string.

When there is an encircled Arabic numeral above or below a note, this indicates which string should be used for that note. In the example, the note would be played on the 2nd string with the 3rd finger (indicated by the 3 next to the note). The note is D, on the 3rd fret and will be learned later.

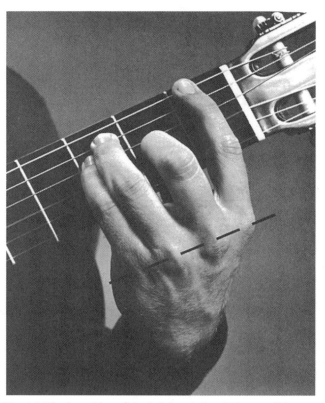

Fig. 24 The knuckles of the left hand should be parallel to the fingerboard.

Fig. 23 Position of the left arm.

With the left hand, grip the neck of the guitar as shown. When the arm hangs in a natural, relaxed manner, it is in the correct position for playing.

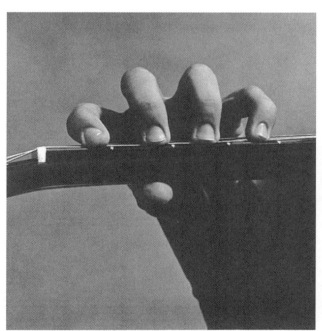

Fig. 25 Position of the thumb.

The left-hand thumb is generally placed midway on the back of the neck in line with the index and middle fingers. The student should be careful that the thumb does not protrude above the fingerboard or neck. Otherwise, you may find that the rest of the hand is, in many cases, out of position.

Positioning of the Left-Hand Fingers

The string should be met by the tip of the finger in most cases, and the nails of the left hand must be cut short enough to allow the fingertips to be in a perpendicular position to the fingerboard when depressing the strings. The thumb applies counter-pressure from behind the neck.

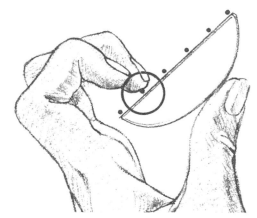

Fig. 26 Playing on the fingertip.

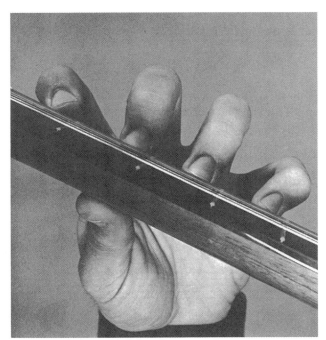

Fig. 27 A balanced left-hand position (top view).

The 1st or index finger should lie slightly on its side.*

The 2nd or middle finger should meet the string in a vertical position.

The 3rd or ring finger should also meet the string in a vertical position.

The 4th or little finger lies slightly on its side in a direction opposite the index finger.

*When moving up the neck, the index finger gradually moves into a vertical position (due to the smaller fret spacing). The other fingers remain as described.

All fingers should form an arch, with the knuckles parallel to the fingerboard. The movement of the finger should begin from the knuckle.

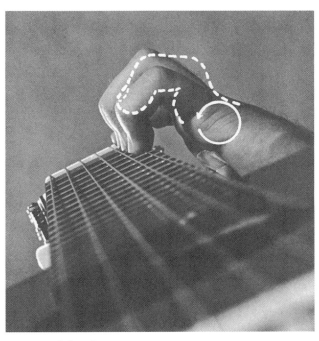

Fig. 28 Left-hand position on treble string.

Fig. 29 Left-hand position on bass string.

When depressing the string, press it firmly, just behind the fret wire to produce a good, clear tone.

For economy of movement and security, never lift a finger unnecessarily after it has played a note.

When the fingers are not depressing a string, keep them hovering comfortably close to the strings and ready to play.

Notes on the 1st or High E String

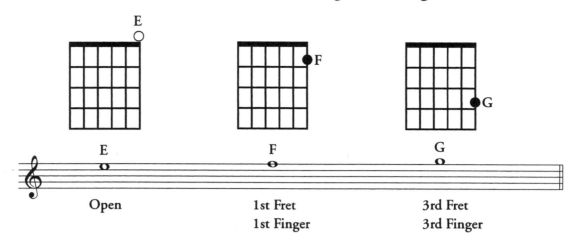

Study #10 Try rest stroke and free stroke. Set your thumb on the 6th string for more security. At the beginning of the 2nd measure, it is a good idea to leave the left-hand 1st finger in place on F when adding your 3rd finger to play the higher note G. Use this technique whenever possible.

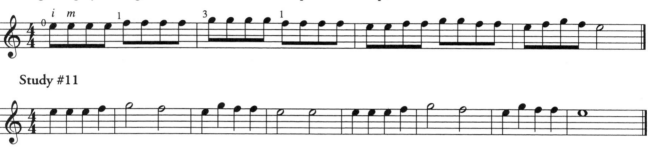

Study #11

As you practice, your left-hand fingertips may become slightly sore. With consistent practice over two or three weeks, you will develop calluses that will protect your fingertips. This will make it easier and more comfortable to depress the strings.

Study #12

DUET FOUR

DUET FIVE

29

Notes on the 2nd or B String

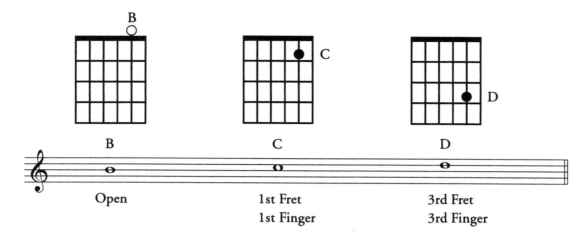

Open   1st Fret   3rd Fret

1st Finger   3rd Finger

Study #13   It is often helpful at first to say the name of the note aloud as you play it.

Study #14

WALTZ IN A MINOR

Use rest stroke on the melody (notes with upward stems) to achieve a fuller sound. Alternation of *i* and *m* is not absolutely necessary at this point.

AIR

J. Haydn

Study #15

DUET SIX

DUET SEVEN
(On a Christmas Theme)

Slowly

Student

Teacher

Notes on the 3rd or G String

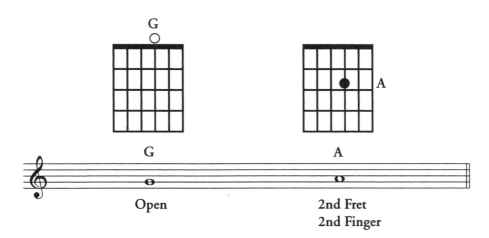

Study #16

Use free stroke throughout the next two pieces.

SPANISH MELODY

PRELUDE IN C MAJOR

Rests

A rest is a symbol indicating silence. These symbols show when not to play. Every note has an equivalent rest in time value which receives the same number of counts. The following chart shows the comparative time value of notes and rests.

Note and Rest Time Values

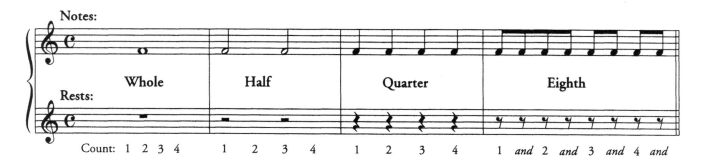

Ties

A tie is a curved line joining two notes of the same pitch. The first note is played and held for the value of two notes without striking the second note. In the following example, both measures will sound identical.

Music in Two Voices

The next solo piece, *Study in Two Voices,* is an example of music in two parts (called *voices*). Generally, the upper treble part (stems up as shown in Ex. A) is the melody, and the lower bass part (stems down as in Ex. B) is the accompaniment. When playing music with two or more voices, be sure to let each note ring for its full time value. This will create an overlapping of voices that often allows the guitar to sound like more than one instrument.

Ex. A Treble Part (Melody)

Ex. B Bass Part (Accompaniment)

STUDY IN TWO VOICES

AU CLAIR DE LA LUNE

OLD FRENCH SONG

The youthful Segovia (seated third from left) listens
intently as the older master Miguel Llobet plays.

Arpeggio

The *arpeggio* (from the Italian "in the manner of a harp") is a very effective technique on the guitar and is used frequently in guitar music. In an arpeggio, the notes of a chord, instead of being played simultaneously, are played one after another. Usually the thumb strikes the down beat (or first beat) of the measure, then the fingers follow in some sequential order, as indicated. An arpeggio is most often played free stroke. The following are examples of arpeggios.

Study #17

Study #18

Planting

Planting is frequently used when playing an arpeggio. It is simply resting or planting the finger or fingers of the right hand on a string prior to playing the string. In other words, you are prepared to play the string before you actually do so.

For most ascending arpeggios (see Study #17), fingers p, i, m, a, may all be placed on the string at the same time and released as the arpeggio ascends. However, when the arpeggio *ascends* and *descends* (as in Study #18), only the ascending part of the arpeggio is

planted. The descending part is played regular free stroke and is not planted. The fingers should not return and plant on the strings until the arpeggio is completed. Generally, the *ima* fingers are planted simultaneously at the moment the thumb starts to play the bass string.

The use of planting will help increase your accuracy and speed when playing arpeggios. Remember to plant all the fingers at the same time, securely and in a position ready for playing.

Arpeggio
DUET EIGHT

Sharps, Flats and Naturals

Sharps, flats and naturals are called chromatic signs (or accidentals). They raise or lower a note by one half-step (or half-tone) which is equal to one fret on the guitar. Once a note is altered by an accidental, it remains that way throughout the measure until it is automatically canceled out by the bar line. Sometimes a natural sign is used in a following measure as a courtesy reminder.

Chromatic Signs

 The *Sharp* raises the note by one half-step.
(C sharp is played on the 2nd fret, 2nd string.)

 The *Flat* lowers the note by one fret.
(D flat is played on the 2nd fret, 2nd string.)*

 The *Natural* restores the note to its regular pitch after it has been raised or lowered.

*C sharp and D flat are called *enharmonic* notes—written differently but sounding the same.

In the following piece, be sure to sharp all the F's by playing them on the 2nd fret of the 1st string. Later in the book, you will see this notated by the use of a key signature (p. 66).

PRELUDE IN G MAJOR

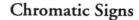

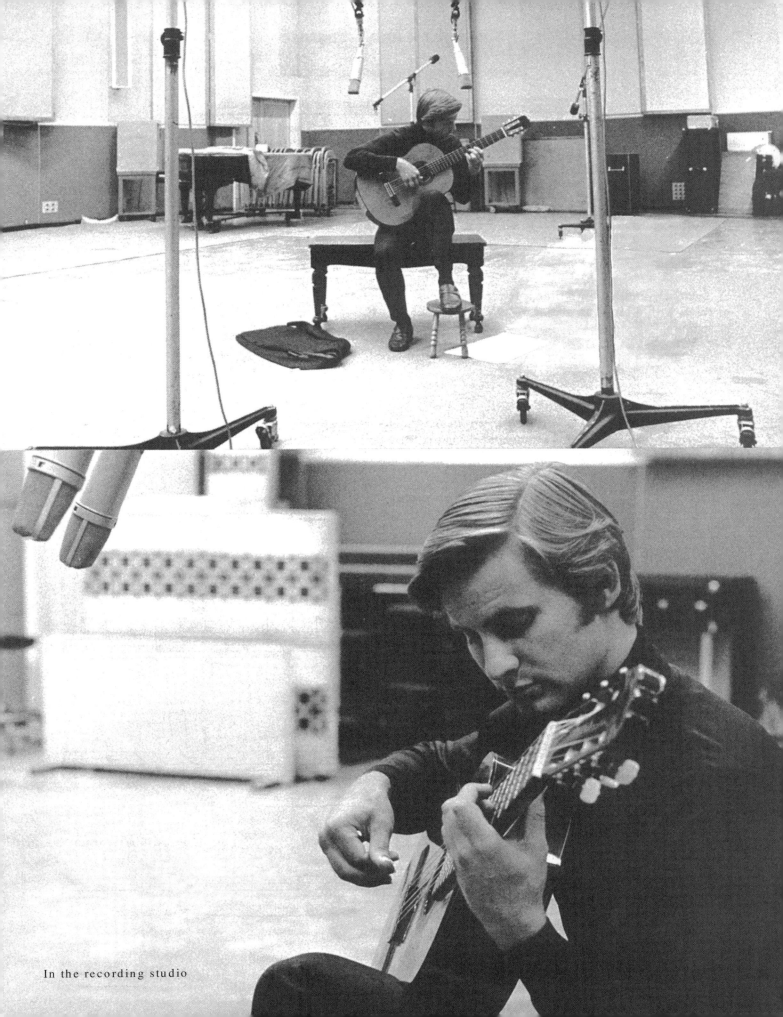

In the recording studio

Six-Eight Time Signature

Another time signature used in music is 6/8.

A dot placed after a quarter note increases the time value of the note by one half: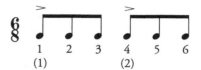

Generally, music in 6/8 time is felt in two groups of three, with a bit of an accent on the first note of each group:

The following piece is an excellent warm-up and should eventually be memorized (see next page). Leave your 2nd finger on the 3rd string *A* throughout the entire piece for left-hand security.

Study #19

Memorization

In general, to perform a piece of music beautifully and accurately, it is essential to devote complete concentration to it. This is not often possible when sight-reading the music; therefore when learning a piece of music it may be necessary, eventually, to commit it to memory.

It is important to know when to memorize. You must be able to play the piece correctly (i.e., notes, fingering, rhythm), before starting to memorize.

After you have played the piece through a number of times, you should have become familiar not only with the shapes and patterns of the left-hand fingers on the fingerboard, but also with the sound of the written music.

To start with, play the piece from the beginning and see how far you can go without looking at the music. When you can go no farther, consult the music. If this refreshes your memory, proceed again without the music; otherwise, play only the section you had forgotten until you have learned it. Now continue without the music again until you can go no farther. Repeat the above procedure until the entire piece is memorized.

Many of the solo pieces in this book should be committed to memory, along with any of the studies recommended by the author or by your teacher, which concentrate on the development of specific techniques.

Memorization is an aid in the development of technique, for it allows full concentration on technical advancement.

DUET NINE

GERMAN FOLK SONG

41

Notes on the 4th or D String

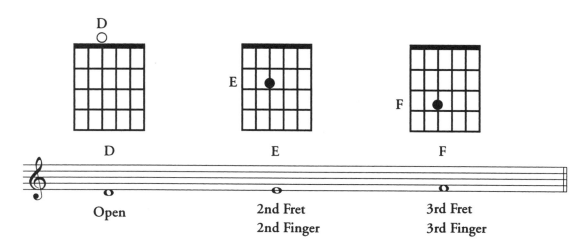

MARCH

Study #20 Use free stroke throughout.

Triplets and Sixteenth Notes

You have already learned that the quarter note can be divided into two equal parts which are called eighth notes. The quarter note may be divided into even smaller parts. If we divide the quarter note into three equal parts, these notes are called *triplets*. A triplet is signified by the numeral 3 above the group of three notes forming the triplet. (Ex. 1) In a series of continuous triplets (as in *Melancolia*) it is not necessary to continue to mark the number 3 on each triplet after the first measure. *Sixteenth* notes are created when you divide a quarter note into four parts. These are twice as fast as eighth notes. (Ex. 2)

Ex. 1 Triplets

Count: 1   2   *and*   3 *and a*

Ex. 2 Sixteenth Notes

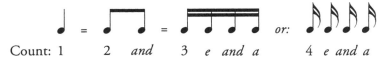

Count: 1   2   *and*   3 *e and a*   *or:*   4 *e and a*

MELANCOLIA

Pick-up Notes

Some pieces of music begin with an incomplete measure. The notes in this measure are called *pick-up notes.* One must work backwards from the end of the measure to see where to start counting. One quarter note in an incomplete measure of 4/4 time would simply be counted "four" (Ex. 3). In other words, the quarter note is the last beat of this measure. The duet on the following page begins with a pick-up note (count "3 – 4" as shown).

Ex. 3 Pick-up Note

Count: 4   1   2   3   4

Duet Ten

FUGUE

JOHANN SEBASTIAN BACH
(1685–1750)

Notes on the 5th or A String

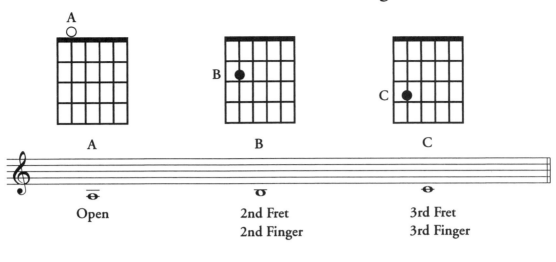

A — Open

B — 2nd Fret / 2nd Finger

C — 3rd Fret / 3rd Finger

TOCCATA

J.S. Bach

MINUET

J.S. Bach

C Major Scale (with variations)*

Use rest stroke.

a) etc.   b) etc.

* For an explanation of scale construction and music theory, refer to p. 66.

Notes on the 6th or Low E String

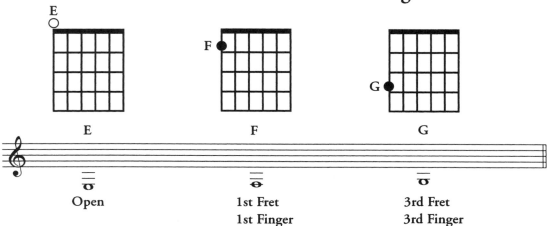

Study #21

FANDANGO

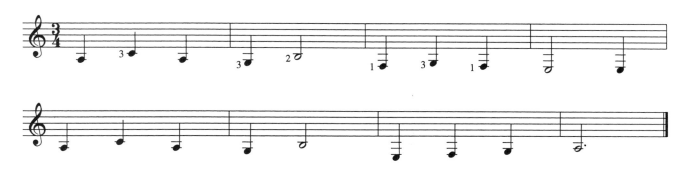

The Natural Scale

The Natural Scale should be studied and memorized. It is a review of all the natural notes (no sharps or flats) learned up to this point.

VARIATION ON A SPANISH THEME

Be sure to let each bass note ring for its full value (until the next bass note).

* In guitar music, the wavy line preceding a chord means to strum the notes of the chord with the thumb.

The Fingernails

I recommend that, at this point, the serious classical guitar student begin to use the nails of the right hand in conjunction with the fleshy part of the fingertips when sounding the strings. When this technique is developed, the student will be able to produce a more beautiful sound, a wider variety of tonal colors, and a greater control of dynamics.

The nails of the right hand should generally follow the contour of the fingertips and should extend about 1/16" to 1/8" of an inch beyond the flesh. (Fig. 30)

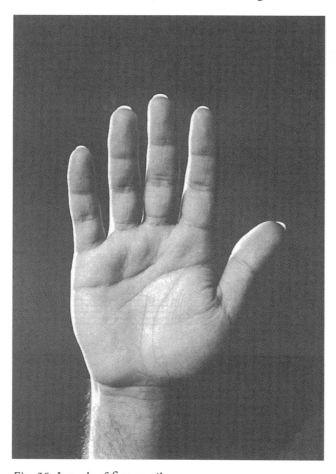

Fig. 30 Length of fingernails.

When properly filed, the nails should glide smoothly over the string.

Five Steps for Filing Nails

The following is a basic guide for filing the nails. Nail and finger characteristics, however, differ with each individual, therefore precise rules regarding the shape of the nails are not possible to make.

1. Use a fine file (such as *Alpha-9™, Revlon™,* or *Diamond Deb™*) to round the nails, leaving approximately 1/16" to 1/8" beyond the flesh of the fingertip. *Follow the contour of your fingertip.* Check for length by holding the fingers perpendicular to the floor at eye level. (Fig. 30)

2. Place the file at a slight angle and flat underneath the nail edge, and again shape the nail edge to form an even, flat surface. This corrects any unevenness around the outer edge of the nail. (Fig. 31)

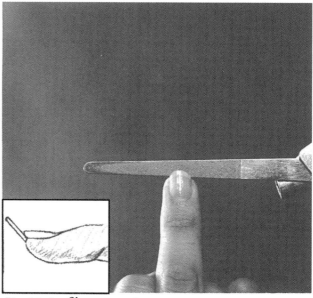

Fig. 31 Set file at an angle.

3. Check the shape of the nail by playing a string. With the finger relaxed, the correctly shaped nail should glide freely across the string. If there is a feeling of hooking or catching during the stroke, the nail has not been properly filed (or the placement of the finger and nail to the string is incorrect. See next page).

4. Use *very fine* sandpaper for polishing the fingernail edges. I use *3M #500 Tri-M-ite™ Fre-Cut* (open coat), available through hardware stores. This step corrects the raspy sound caused by the rough edges after filing.

5. Now, listen to the tone as you strike the string. If it is harsh or unpleasant to the ear, repolish the fingernail edges with the finishing paper until the sound is clear and beautiful. A sound with a slight scrape or raspiness should be avoided. Listen to the recordings of Andrés Segovia for an example of beautiful tone production and control.

Each student will, by experimenting over a period of time, find the best procedure for keeping his nails in the most advantageous playing conditions.

When a nail splits or cracks, nail glue or a silk-wrap may be used for a quick repair. Colorless enamel or nail polish also helps to protect the nail against damage. Apply the enamel to the entire nail, and then remove that which adheres to the outer edge of the fingernail tip with nail polish remover; otherwise the enamel will make a scratchy sound on the string.

For more detailed information on nail filing, see Appendix A in *The Christopher Parkening Method Book, Volume Two.*

Tone Production

Finger and Nail Placement

At this point, it is assumed that the student is now using the fingernail to produce a sound. The proper placement of the finger and nail to the string is very important. (Fig. 32)

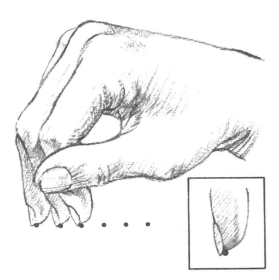

Fig. 32 Correct finger placement.

Producing a good sound or tone is achieved by a combination of both nail and flesh. Nail alone produces a tin-like sound, good only for certain effects. Most important: For round, full, beautiful tone, pad and nail should touch the string simultaneously at the initial point of contact. The stroke should begin on the side of the fingernail (point of contact) and should ride toward the center (point of release). (Fig. 33) The point of contact is where the fingertip, fingernail, and string meet simultaneously before activating the string. This is generally toward the left-hand side of the fingernail (the side closest to the thumb).

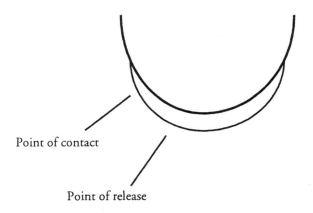

Point of contact

Point of release

Fig. 33 Point of Contact (combination nail and flesh).

A stroke with the thumbnail will generally be made with the thumb at roughly a 45° angle from the string. The stroke should begin near the center of the nail and should ride toward the left side of the nail to release.

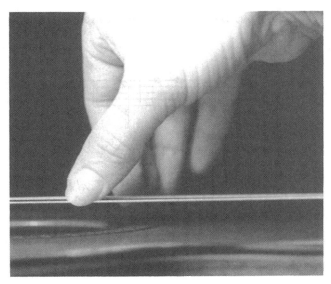

Fig. 34 Correct thumb position.

If there is a feeling of catching, or the sound of a clicking noise, as the string comes in contact with the finger, then one of two things may be wrong: 1) the nail may be too long or improperly filed, or 2) the fingers i, m, a, which should be almost perpendicular to the strings, may be slanting too much to one side, forcing the nail to touch the string before the flesh is able to deaden the clicking sound.

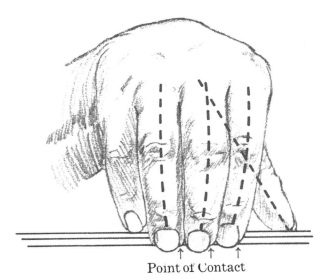

Point of Contact

Fig. 35 Fingers should be almost perpendicular to string.

Always listen carefully to the sound you are producing. Beautiful sound production will take some individual experimentation and refinement as you proceed through your studies. For more on this subject, see Appendix A in *The Christopher Parkening Method Book, Volume Two*.

Two Notes Played Together

When playing two notes together with the thumb and a finger, use a pinching motion as the thumb and finger close toward each other. When playing two notes with two fingers, bring both fingers toward the palm of the hand as a unit. Be sure not to pluck in an outward motion. Do not let the bass notes over-power the melody notes.

In the following piece, the term *D.C. al Fine* means return to the beginning of the piece and play until the end of the measure marked *Fine*.

SPANISH DANCE

KINGS OF ORIENT

50

A Segovia master class.

At the author's Spanish concert debut.

Open String Equivalents

The following diagram illustrates an alternate way of playing notes normally found on open strings (5th through 1st). The arabic numeral enclosed in a circle always denotes the string on which a note is to be played. Compare this with the tuning diagram on p. 13.

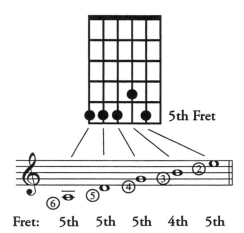

In the following piece, the encircled "3" indicates that the B is to be played on the 3rd string instead of the usual 2nd string.

DUET ELEVEN
Old French Air*

*This duet is written in the form of a canon or round. Both parts have the same melody throughout, although starting at different points.

Guide and Pivot Fingers

The following piece contains two techniques that facilitate left-hand movement. Between measures one and two, leave your 1st and 2nd fingers on the strings as you move up two frets to the B and D in the following measure. When you move a finger while keeping it on the string, it is called a *guide* finger. Be sure to release the pressure slightly to avoid a sliding sound. Between measures five and six, leave the 2nd finger in place on the A when you change chords. This is called a *pivot* or *anchor* finger.

PRELUDE IN A MINOR

Fine

D.C. al Fine

CHROMATIC SCALE (in G)

The chromatic scale consists entirely of notes one fret apart. This scale can be used to create a variety of finger dexterity and coordination exercises. The following study is a one-octave chromatic scale based on G.

Study #22

53

Guitarist-composer-conductor Jack Marshall.

On the following two pieces, strive to let each note ring for its entire duration.

THEME FROM SYMPHONY NO. 9

LUDWIG VAN BEETHOVEN
(1770–1827)

ENGLISH FOLK SONG

ANONYMOUS

Table of Common Tempo Terms

The following Italian expression marks are often found at the beginning of a piece of music to indicate the tempo (or speed) of the piece. They are listed here from slowest to fastest and are all relative. They do not signify an absolute rate of speed.

Lento	Slowly
Andante	Gracefully, a walking tempo
Andantino	Generally interpreted as a bit faster than Andante
Moderato	Moderately
Allegretto	Moderately fast
Allegro	Quickly
Presto	Very Quickly

Here are some other terms to indicate a change of tempo:

Ritardando (*rit.*)	Gradually slower
Accelerando (*accel.*)	Gradually faster
Fermata (⌒)	Hold a note longer than its original value
A Tempo	Return to original tempo
Rubato	Freely slowing down or speeding up

Dynamic Markings

Dynamic markings indicate the volume of a particular passage of music. These terms are also relative, and as with all expressive devices, it is ultimately the performer's decision, taking into account the composer's wishes, as to the interpretation of a piece of music.

pp (*pianissimo*)	Very soft
p (*piano*)	Soft
mp (*mezzo-piano*)	Moderately soft
mf (*mezzo-forte*)	Moderately loud
f (*forte*)	Loud
ff (*fortissimo*)	Very loud
Crescendo	Gradually louder
Decrescendo (also *diminuendo*)	Gradually softer

Repeat Markings

D.C. al Fine	Return to the beginning and play to the *Fine*.
D.S. al Fine	Return to the 𝄋 and play to the *Fine*.
D.C. al Coda	Return to the beginning, play to the ⊕ and skip to the *Coda*.
D.S. al Coda	Return to the 𝄋, play to the ⊕ and skip to the *Coda*.

Multiple Endings: Play until the repeat sign and the return to the facing repeat sign (beginning of piece). On the second time through, skip the 1st ending and instead play the 2nd ending.

ALLEGRO

MAURO GIULIANI
(1781–1828)

Although the interpretation of music depends on individual decisions by the performer, often the composer will add expression markings in the music. Sometimes they are added by the transcriber or editor, as is the case in this next piece. Use them as suggestions from which to develop your own interpretation.

ODE TO JOY

Ludwig van Beethoven
(1770–1827)

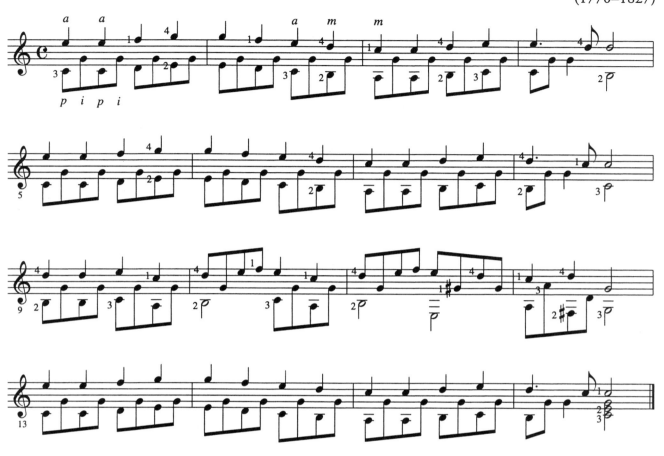

SPANISH WALTZ

ANDANTINO

MATTEO CARCASSI
(1770–1841)

Study #23 This chromatic scale study is an excellent technique builder. Alternate *i* and *m*. Try using *ia* and *ma* also. You may leave your left-hand fingers in place as you ascend each string for security.

Duet Twelve
IN THE HALL OF MOUNTAIN KING
(from the *Peer Gynt* Suite)

EDVARD GREIG

Three Notes Played Together

Three notes may be played at the same time by using the fingers i, m, a, or by using the thumb and two fingers (ie. *p,i,m*). The melody note of the chord should be emphasized. Try both fingerings on this next piece.

HYMN

ESTUDIO*

DIONISIO AGUADO
(1784–1849)

*This piece may be used as a three-note chord study by changing each arpeggio into a chord.

High A on the 1st String

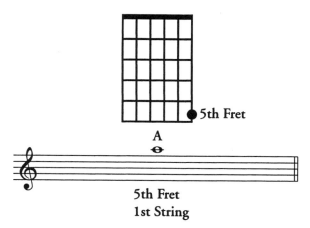

5th Fret
A
5th Fret
1st String

The A on the 5th fret, 1st string is in unison with the A–440 tuning fork. It is the highest note used in Volume One of this method book.

TARANTELLA

SICILIAN TRADITIONAL

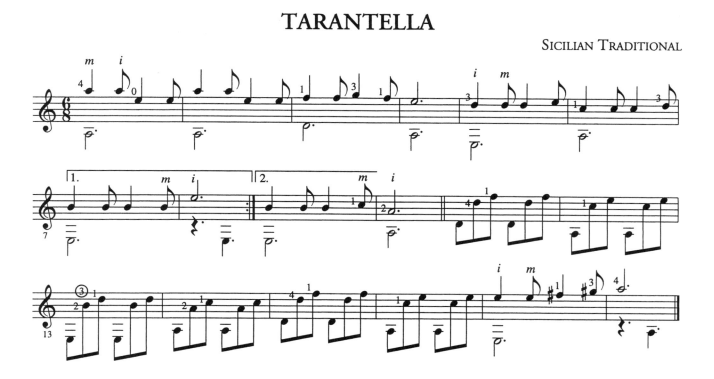

Study #24 The low C in this piece is called a *pedal tone* (a constant note around which other voices move). It is held with the 3rd finger throughout the entire piece.

Duet Thirteen
BOURRÉE

JOHANN SEBASTIAN BACH
(1685–1750)

Four Notes Played Together

The free stroke is most often used when playing four-note chords. The right hand should be relaxed with all the movement coming from the thumb and fingers. In playing four-part chords, the melody is usually the top note and therefore is sounded by the *a* finger. Strive for a good *balance* between all the notes with the melody note clearly defined.

The sharp at the beginning of each line in the next piece is called a *key signature*. It requires that you sharp all F's in the piece, regardless of the octave in which they occur. For more about this topic, see p. 66.

INTERMEZZO

PRELUDE IN C MAJOR*

MATTEO CARCASSI
(1770–1841)

Try planting before each arpeggio.

*This piece may be used as a four-note chord study by changing each arpeggio into a chord.

64

In the following piece, you may *roll* or *arpeggiate* a chord occasionally for a nice musical effect. This involves playing the notes from the bass to the treble (thumb to the *a* finger) in rapid succession. This will broaden the chord. You should start playing the chord slightly early so that the last note (melody note) will land on the beat.

GREENSLEEVES

ANONYMOUS

Music Theory

In studying classical guitar, it is wise to understand the basic mechanics of music theory. The very simple material presented here will start you on the path to grasping the systematic principles of music and will be very helpful to you in the studies to follow.

Intervals

An *interval* is the distance in pitch between two musical tones. The smallest type of interval is a *half-step* (or *half tone*)—one fret on the guitar. A *whole-step* is the next smallest interval. It is equal to two half-steps—two frets on the guitar. Another common interval in music is the *octave*. This is eight letters away from another note of the same name (e.g. C D E F G A B C). On the guitar, octaves are 12 frets apart if played on the same string.

Major Scales

Classical music, in fact almost all music in the Western culture, is based on the *diatonic major scale*. This scale is composed of seven different consecutive notes with an eighth additional note an octave higher than the first note or *root*. Every major scale is constructed the same way with the whole-steps and half-steps in the same order.

You have already learned a C major scale. Examine the intervals. Notice the half-steps between B and C and E and F:

C Major Scale

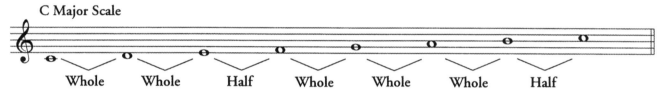

If we start on the 5th note of the C major scale, we may construct a G major scale using the same formula. Notice that we must sharp the F to maintain the same relationship of half-steps and whole-steps.

G Major Scale

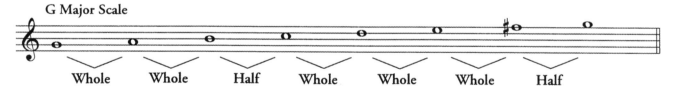

Key Signatures

When playing music in keys that require sharps or flats to construct the major scale, you will find a *key signature* at the beginning of each staff, immediately following the clef sign. This signifies the notes that are to be flat or sharp throughout the entire piece, unless canceled by a natural sign. Always remember to sharp or flat the notes in whatever octave they appear, not just where they are marked in the key signature. For instance, in the key of G major you would sharp the F on the 1st string, 2nd fret; the 4th string, 4th fret; and the 6th string, 2nd fret (see example at right).

Key of G Major

Sharp all F's

Here are the most common key signatures found in guitar music:

C Major	G Major	D Major	A Major	E Major	F Major
(A minor)	(E minor)	(B minor)	(F♯ minor)	(C♯ minor)	(D minor)

Music Theory (cont.)

Circle of Fifths

There are 15 Major Keys: One with no sharps or flats, and then seven sharp keys and seven flat keys. The *Circle of Fifths* is a useful visual aid to help remember the proper order of keys with all their sharps and flats. The key of C major appears on top with no sharps or flats. Going clockwise, you will find the Sharp keys: Key of G (1 sharp), Key of D (2 sharps), Key of A (3 sharps), etc., all the way around to the Key of C♯ (7 sharps). Going counter-clockwise from the Key of C, you will find the Flat keys: Key of F (1 flat), Key of B♭ (2 flats), Key of E♭ (3 flats), etc., all the way around to the Key of C♭ (7 flats).

Note: The keys of B, F♯, and C♯ have *enharmonic* equivalents: C♭, G♭, and D♭. These keys are written differently but sound the same.

The order of sharps and flats is listed below the circle. Reading from left to right, if a piece has two sharps they would be F and C. If it has three sharps, they would be F, C and G. If a piece has one flat it would be B, and a piece with three flats would contain B, E, and A. As the key signatures progress around the circle of 5ths, they always contain the previous key's sharps or flats.

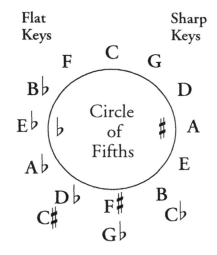

Order of Sharps: F C G D A E B

Order of Flats: B E A D G C F

Relative Minors

Every major key has a relative minor key which shares its key signature, scale tones, and chords. To find the relative minor for any major key, descend 1½ steps (3 frets) from the major key root. This is actually the 6th tone in the major scale. For example: The relative minor for C is A minor (C and A are 3 frets apart, and A is the 6th tone in the C major scale). A piece of music with the key signature of no sharps and flats would either be in the key of C major or A minor. The last chord of the piece will usually indicate the key.

Chords

Chord construction can be somewhat complicated for the beginning student, but simple chords are easy to understand. Chords are derived from the major scale. Most chords are built on a three note chord called a *triad*. To build a *major* triad, you take the root, 3rd, and 5th from the major scale. (Ex. 1) To change this to a *minor* triad, simply flat the third of the chord. (Ex. 2) Chords may be *voiced* in a variety of ways. Example 3 shows various voicings of the C major chord. The only requirement here is that the chord contain at least one root, 3rd, and 5th.

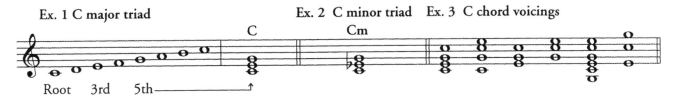

For more on chord voicings, refer to the chord chart in the Appendix.

Transposing Keys

Pieces can be written in every key, but some keys are more adaptable to the guitar than others. This folk song, for example, is written here in the key of C (no sharps or flats). It has also been *transposed* to the key of A (3 sharps) and B♭ (2 flats). These three adaptations are for illustrating keys only and need not be practiced.

AMERICAN FOLK SONG

In the Key of C:

In the Key of A:

In the Key of B♭:

The author conducting his Master Class at the University of Southern California.

Christopher Parkening and co-author David Brandon on stage at Queen Elizabeth Hall (London, England).

Three Technical Exercises

I consider the following three studies most valuable. When properly learned, they will maintain the techniques covered thus far in this book. Strive for full round tones, and remember, as always, to practice relaxed. For extra arpeggio practice, I recommend *120 Studies for the Right Hand* by Mauro Giuliani.

This Chromatic Study in triplets by Tárrega is excellent for developing facility of the left hand and speed of the right-hand rest stroke. Practice with the metronome, and gradually increase your speed. I recommend starting with the metronome set at 80, with one click per note. Try to increase your speed to a goal of 160. Remember to rest firmly against the adjacent string when playing the rest stroke, and use the adjacent string as a sort of "springboard" in returning the fingers to their playing position. When striving for speed, stay relaxed yet push yourself for more endurance with accuracy.

CHROMATIC STUDY

FRANCISCO TÁRREGA
(1852–1909)

The following arpeggio series is commonly found in guitar music. Practice it using free stroke. The planting technique may also be used. Steadily increase your speed as you are able.

Study #25

This next study on a well-known arpeggio Etude will help improve the right-hand free stroke technique. Play it repeatedly, practicing both sets of right-hand fingerings, and steadily work up to a fast speed.

Study #26

Duet Fourteen
BOURRÉE

George Philipp Telemann
(1681–1767)

Bourrée (cont.)

The Bar

The bar is a required part of guitar technique. It means to depress more than one string simultaneously on a single fret with the first or index finger of the left hand. It is used to facilitate fingering, most often as an easier way of fingering two or more notes on the same fret. (Fig. 36)

Fig. 36 The full bar (front view).

Forming the bar:

1. Keep left-hand thumb low on the neck to apply counter-pressure. It should maintain a natural position opposite the index and middle fingers.

2. Keep the bar finger (index) as close to the fret as possible.

3. The index finger generally presses somewhat on the side of the finger. (Fig. 37) This usually works best with the side closest to the thumb, although for some bars, the opposite side may be effective.

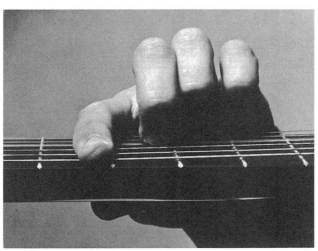

Fig. 37 The full bar (top view).

If the notes in your bar do not sound clear, you might try the following:

• Try adjusting the bar vertically up or down. In other words, you may wish to use a 1/2 bar instead of a 1/3 bar. Even with a full bar, there is room to move the finger vertically one way or the other. This may allow the finger to put pressure in a different area, producing a clear sound.

• Focus the pressure directly on the string or strings that are unclear. Usually the outer strings (top and bottom of the bar) will be clear. You may need extra pressure in the middle of the finger.

• Make sure to sit with the guitar tilted slightly backward. In this position, you have the advantage of gravity with the weight of the left arm to help the bar.

• If only the outer strings are needed in the bar chord, you may curve the bar slightly, allowing the inner strings to be muted. Therefore, you only apply pressure where it is necessary.

• Play through a passage even though the bar might not be totally clear. Play the bar chord anyway and keep on going. Later practice the bar chord separately. If you spend too long on any one chord, your finger may become fatigued and the bar will be even harder.

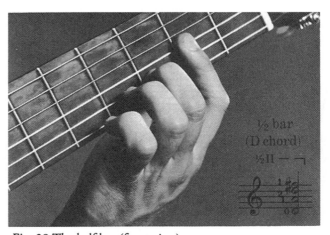

Fig. 38 The half bar (front view).

Strength does play an important role in bar chords, but correct finger and thumb placement are equally important. It is often the case of position rather than pressure. With practice, you will begin to produce a clear, ringing sound from each string without undue pressure from the left hand.

For more advanced barring techniques, see *The Christopher Parkening Method Book, Volume Two.*

The Bar (cont.)

Notating the bar:

There is some discrepancy when it comes to bar chord notation. In this method book and in all my arrangements, we use a Roman numeral to indicate the fret on which to use a full bar. (Ex. A) A partial bar is indicated by a Roman numeral preceded by a fraction telling how many strings to bar. (Ex. B)

Other bar terminology you might encounter involves the use of a capital C (*cejilla* in Spanish) or a capital B (*barre* in French) placed before the Roman numeral indicating the fret. A "c" with a vertical line through it would mean a partial bar. (Ex. C) Arabic numbers are even occasionally used instead of Roman numerals.

The bar is held for the value of the note or notes it produces. This is generally indicated by a line above the staff following the Roman numeral. (Ex. D)

Ex. A Full Bar   Ex. B Half Bar

Ex. C Alternate notation

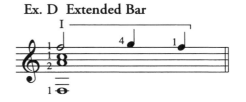

Ex. D Extended Bar

PRELUDE IN D MAJOR

ALL THROUGH THE NIGHT

WELSH AIR

Tárrega playing for a gathering of friends.

Supplementary

Pieces

The following supplementary pieces will help you build technique and refine your musical skills. They are arranged by key rather than by difficulty, although the easier keys are placed first. At this point, the student may also proceed to *The Christopher Parkening Method Book, Volume Two*, while still developing repertoire from the last section of this book.

Key of C Major

MODERATO

Mauro Giuliani

ENGLISH DANCE

Matteo Carcassi

D.C. al Fine

RONDO

JEAN-PHILIPPE RAMEAU
(1683–1764)

ANDANTE

FERNANDO SOR
(1778–1839)

Key of A Minor

ETUDE

FERDINAND CARULLI
(1792–1853)

D.C. al Fine

PACKINGTON'S POUND

ANONYMOUS

FÜR ELISE

LUDWIG VAN BEETHOVEN

Key of G Major

SCOTTISH FOLK SONG

TRADITIONAL

MINUET IN G

JOHANN SEBASTIAN BACH
(1685–1750)

LULLABY

JOHANNES BRAHMS
(1833–1897)

Key of E Minor

WALTZ IN E MINOR

FERDINAND CARULLI
(1792–1853)

Key of D Major
SIMPLE GIFTS

ANONYMOUS

Allegro

MINUET

ROBERT DE VISÉE
(circa 1660–1720)

Andante

KEMP'S JIG

Anonymous

Key of D Minor

ITALIAN DANCE

Hans Neusiedler
(1508–1563)

Key of A Major

BOURRÉE

Johann Sebastian Bach
(1685–1750)

Moderato

THEME

George Frederic Handel
(1685–1759)

Allegretto

Three Spanish Encores

SPANISH FOLK SONG

TRADITIONAL

D.C. al Fine

CATALONIAN SONG

SPANISH FOLK SONG

MALAGUEÑA

TRADITIONAL

JESU, JOY OF MAN'S DESIRING
from Cantata No. 147

J.S. Bach

Appendix

Performing with the Washington, D.C.,National Symphony.

Rehearsing with the Los Angeles Philharmonic.

Summary of Guitar Music Fingering

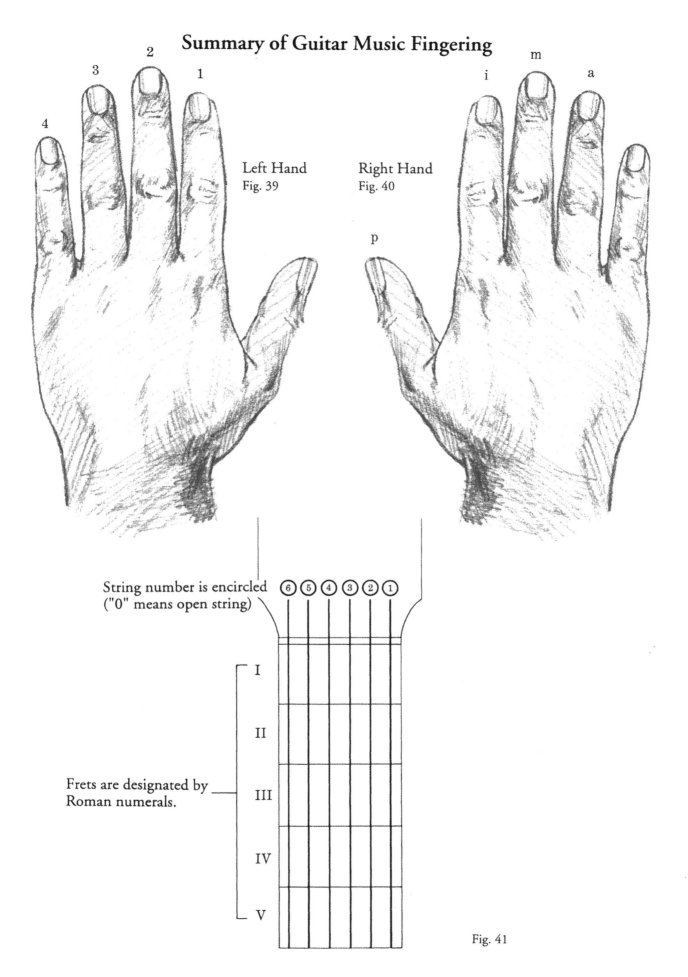

Left Hand
Fig. 39

Right Hand
Fig. 40

String number is encircled
("0" means open string)

⑥ ⑤ ④ ③ ② ①

Frets are designated by
Roman numerals.

I

II

III

IV

V

Fig. 41

The Classical Guitar: A Brief History

The beginnings of the guitar are buried deep within the pages of history. Archeologists say that the earliest musical instruments were primitive percussion devices which date back almost to the creation of man. Stringed instruments, too, have a long ancestry, many of which are mentioned in the Bible. The first may have been conceived by some early huntsman who liked the sound made when he plucked his hunting bow. To it, one might have added a sounding chest made of an empty tortoise shell or gourd.

The guitar as we know it today was developed in Western Europe, though nobody can say precisely where or when. Its direct ancestors included the chetarah of the Assyrians, the kinnura of the Hebrews, the qitra of the Chaldeans, the sitar of India, the ki-tar ("three strings") of Egypt, the kithara of the Greeks, and the oud (later translated *laud* and eventually, *lute*) of Persia, which was carried in 711 A.D. by the conquering Moors into Southern Spain. Gypsies wandering west from Persia and, in the 12th Century, Crusaders returning from the East to Europe, brought early versions of the lute and vihuela. From these instruments, by a continuous process of experimentation and modification, evolved the guitar.

Some historians say it made its first appearance in Spain, the country with which it has long been associated. In these early manifestations, and indeed until the middle of the 17th Century, it was apt to be strung with four or five pairs of double strings, called *courses*. These instruments are known today as the Renaissance guitar or Baroque guitar. The existence of these instruments and its music was first seen in the vihuela methods of Alonso Mudarra (1546), Miguel Fuenllana (1554) and later, especially the five-course guitar, throughout the Baroque era, gaining popularity in many Western European countries. By 1790, this instrument began to wane and the six single-stringed guitar now gained notoriety. The addition of a lower E string provided the harmonic emphasis needed to perform the classical music of the period. And, with the innovations in fan-strutting (created by the Spanish school of luthiers) and mechanical tuning gears, it was destined for both great musical works and virtuosos at the beginning of the 19th century.

The first great figure to give the guitar the respectability of the concert hall and to reveal it for the infinitely subtle, virtuosic instrument it is, was Fernando Sor (1778–1839). Born in Barcelona, Sor was already an acclaimed accomplished guitarist and composer at 17. In 1797, he went to Madrid, in 1812 to Paris, in 1815 to London, and in the 1820's to Germany and Russia. Everywhere he won astonished admiration for his artistry and new respect for his instrument. Throughout his lifetime, he tirelessly performed, taught, and composed works which became the foundation for the future literature to follow and which are still studied by every serious guitar student today. Sor also wrote a *Method pour las guitare*.

Fernando Sor

Outstanding contemporaries of Sor were his friend Dionisio Aguado (1784–1849) of Madrid, and the Italians Ferdinand Carulli (1792–1853), Matteo Carcassi (1770–1841), and Mauro Giuliani (1781–1828). Aguado, said to have been an even more brilliant virtuoso than Sor, also wrote a method and several volumes of studies for the guitar, including advanced pieces that only a very accomplished guitarist could play. Carulli, born in Naples, won a great reputation in Europe as a performer. In 1808, he settled in Paris and stayed there until his death, teaching, playing, and composing hundreds of works for the guitar, including a method which is still published today. Matteo Carcassi, a Florentine, replaced Carulli as the reigning guitarist of Paris. His "Complete Method," a revision of the Carulli work, contributed many ingenious new ideas to guitar playing which expanded the resources of the instrument. Carcassi composed many favorite studies for the guitar.

Giuliani, a Bolognese, made Vienna his home for many years. He was a friend of Beethoven, and wrote many popular concert pieces, including his *Concerto in A Major* for Guitar and Orchestra.

With the passing of these artists, interest in the guitar fell into a decline. The Romantic period demanded the attention of a guitar luthier with new ideas. Antonio de Torres (1817–1892) provided this by adding the most important refinements to our present day guitar. Having built an estimated 320 guitars, he increased the area of the soundbox, changed the overall proportions, and utilized fan-strutting for bracing thinner woods.

The popularity of the guitar was revived when virtuoso Francisco Tárrega (1854–1909) began to construct his legendary reputation. Born of poor parents in Villareal, Tárrega learned to play guitar from a blind musician while working as a child laborer in a rope factory. The instrument became his great love. After touring Europe with acclaim as a young man, he returned to Spain to devote himself to teaching and to perfecting a technique which has become the foundation of modern guitar playing. In addition to composing his own music, Tárrega adapted for the guitar works by Bach and other great masters. Along with his predecessor Sor and his successor Segovia, Tárrega took his place as one of the great patriarchs of our instrument who have brought the guitar to its respected status today.

Andrés Segovia (1893–1987), born in Linares, was of course, the towering guitar genius of the 20th century. He devoted his lifetime singlemindedly to the advancement of his instrument, securing its acceptance on the concert stage worldwide. Considered beyond doubt the greatest classical guitarist who ever lived, he generously encouraged every promising student who sought his help. It is safe to say that no major guitarist exists who has not been profoundly influenced by him. He inspired a school of modern composers to create a substantial body of new guitar music, among them Rodrigo, Torroba, Turina, Ponce, Roussel, Tansman, Mompou, Duarte, Villa-Lobos, Castelnuovo-Tedesco, and many more. Segovia himself composed and transcribed an invaluable library of guitar works, and he was the most enthusiastic, the most determined, and the most effective proponent for the guitar in its history to date.

So virtually synonymous are "Segovia" and "guitar" that one cannot pronounce either word without thinking simultaneously of the other. Andrés Segovia was quite unashamedly loved by everyone who cherishes the instrument itself.

The guitar today is the most popular instrument in the world, and in many ways, is its own universe still awaiting exploration, still promising many further revelations in years to come.

Francisco Tárrega

Andrés Segovia

Selecting a Classical Guitar

Choosing an instrument of the quality necessary to learn to play properly may present a problem to the beginner. When possible one should obtain the advice and assistance of a fine guitarist or qualified teacher. If neither is available, the following information should be helpful to the student who is buying his or her first guitar.

Generally, the finest classical guitars are made by individual luthiers, and they are typically made with the following woods: the back and sides of rosewood; the top, or soundboard, of a close, even grained cedar or spruce; the neck of cedar or mahogany, and the fingerboard of ebony. It is not necessary for the beginner to buy an extremely expensive guitar. It is, however, most important to make certain that the guitar is in good playing condition.

The standard width of the fingerboard should be between 2" and 2⅛" at the nut (see diagram p. 8). A narrower fingerboard should be avoided for classical playing. The fingerboard should have a slight length-wise concave bow, known as relief. Under no circumstances should the fingerboard have a convex bow or hump. One can get a general idea of the neck's condition by visually sighting down the neck from the head. The frets should be well seated in their slots, smoothly finished, and of equal height. There should not be any sharp edges on the frets.

Every instrument varies from another in sound. After making sure that the guitar is tuned to correct pitch, strum the strings with the thumb of your right hand and listen to the tone of the instrument. Then, to check the quality and evenness of each note, play all the notes up the fingerboard starting with the first string, paying attention to strike the string with even playing pressure. Each note should ring clear (no buzzing) and the volume and duration of each note should be about the same (no wolf or dead notes).

To assure that the guitar is correctly intonated (i.e., the fretted and open notes play in tune), compare the pitch of the open first string with that same string fretted at the 12th fret. The two notes should be the same, only an octave apart. If the open and fretted notes are not in tune, this could most likely be due to a defective string. Repeat this same process for the remaining strings. (Other rare structural problems that may cause intonation problems include a warped fingerboard or misaligned frets.)

The action, or playability of the guitar, which is affected by both the nut and the saddle, should also be checked. If the strings are too high over the fingerboard (high or hard action), the student will

experience difficulty in depressing them firmly against the frets. If the strings are too low over the fingerboard, they will often produce unpleasant buzzing sounds. This is called a low or soft action. Either of these extremes is to be avoided. When the guitar is in proper adjustment, the strings will not be too difficult to depress against the frets and they should produce a clear tone with maximum volume. Height adjustments can be made by the student but the job is much better left to the experienced repairman or guitar maker.

It is a good idea to carefully look over the entire guitar inside and out, if possible, to assure that there are no compromises to the structural integrity of the instrument, such as cracks or loose braces, or even areas where the finish is damaged. Check the tuning pegs to assure that they turn smoothly, without any backlash or resistance.

Finally, and most importantly, select the guitar which sounds the most beautiful to you.

Note: If you are left-handed and have not yet purchased a guitar, I would recommend buying a "right-handed" instrument. While there may be exceptions, it is generally more practical to play right-handed since both hands perform intricate functions and the construction of most guitars is designed for right-handed players.

Care of the Guitar

Every year, the newspapers print stories of some famous, fine old violin, made by Guarneri or Stradivari in the 1600's or 1700's, which has just been sold or auctioned for hundreds of thousands of dollars. Seldom, however, is there any word of the sale of a fine old guitar. One reason is that guitar design and construction have improved so dramatically through the years that all of the most superb sounding instruments have been created recently, in our own century. Another is that due to the construction of the guitar, it is a more vulnerable instrument than the violin and is therefore, not long-lived. As a plucked instrument, the thin soundboard of the guitar is subjected to a substantial amount of wear and tear. It is the hours of playing the instrument, not its age, that cause a guitar to fatigue or wear out.

The longer you own your guitar, the greater your affection for it will deepen, and you will find yourself naturally protective of it. Fortunately, there are measures you can take to protect it and prolong its life.

The first indispensable step is to provide it with a sturdy, well-structured, well-fitted, and well-lined case. Keep your guitar in the case, lid closed *and fastened* at all times when you are not actually playing it.

Never expose your guitar, in or out of the case, to direct sunlight or to sudden or extreme changes of temperature or humidity. The guitar is highly sensitive to all the elements, and any or all of them may cause its wood to crack, its finish to mar, or its neck to warp. Avoid putting your guitar in the trunk of a car.

A guitar's prolonged exposure to very high humidity, or extremely dry weather is potentially destructive. Guard your guitar from heating or air-conditioning which drastically affect the relative humidity of the environment. The problem here is that as a guitar's wood absorbs or loses moisture, it will undergo dimensional changes. When a guitar is subjected to an environment that is much lower in relative humidity than the environment in which it was constructed, the wood will shrink, creating stress within the instrument. This can result in separation of the glue joints, or even cracks in the wood. As the fretboard shrinks, the frets will begin to protrude, or extend beyond edges of the fingerboard a bit. A humidifier, kept in the pocket of the case, or in the instrument itself, can help prevent this. Note that too much humidity will cause the guitar's wood to swell, which can result in a "tubby" sound and even a slightly raised action.

When changing strings, avoid sudden, total relaxation of string tension exerted on the bridge by changing only one string at a time. This precaution maintains a relatively steady tension, allowing the guitar to stay in tune more quickly once the new strings are installed. If, however, the guitar is not to be played for a period of several months or more, prevent strain on the bridge by loosening all six strings so that there is no string tension on the bridge, until such time as you begin to play again. Also, do not subject your guitar to excessively high tuning. Avoid a pitch higher than the standard A–440 for long periods of time.

To keep the guitar's finish clean and glossy, rub it with a soft, slightly damp cloth, or occasionally apply sparingly a reputable polish made specifically for guitar. Always protect your guitar from elements which can mar its finish. If the guitar has not consistently been kept inside its case when not being played, it can accumulate dust which will attract moisture. If, despite all precautions, damage to your guitar does occur, take it immediately to a qualified repair expert.

Attaching Strings

1. Lay the guitar on its back with the neck on the left-hand side.

2. Put one end of the string through the horizontal bridge hole. There should remain approximately 1½ inches of string on the right side of the bridge. (See Fig. 42)

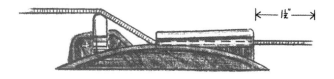

Fig. 42

3. Wrap this 1½" of string around itself twice, allowing the remainder to come out behind the bridge. (Fig. 43)

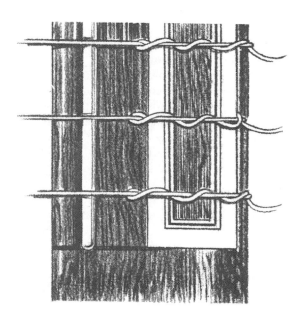

Fig. 43

4. The other end of the string is pulled up towards the head over the nut and placed in its proper slot. (Fig. 44)

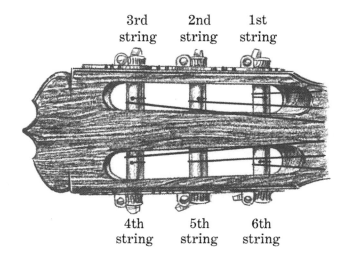

3rd string 2nd string 1st string

4th string 5th string 6th string

Fig. 44

5. Then it is passed through the hole in the roller and pulled over and under itself twice around. Hold this end of the string until the string is secured. (See Fig. 45)

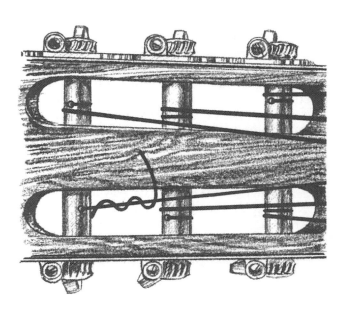

Fig. 45

6. Carefully cut the excess at both ends of the string to avoid buzzing.

Guitar Chord Chart

While chords are a basic element of many classical pieces, they are essential for accompaniment in popular styles of music. Experiment with different chord progressions using various strum and arpeggio patterns. Try creating your own chord variations by adding or subtracting one or more fingers. To expand your knowledge of chords and harmony, obtain a good chord dictionary.

Basic Open Chords

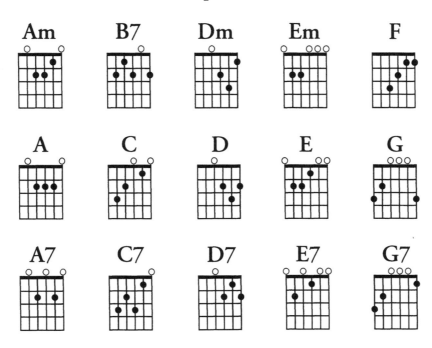

Moveable Bar Chords

Bar chords are moveable horizontally along the fingerboard because they contain no open strings. The two charts on the left show at which fret to bar the index finger to achieve a desired chord. For instance, if you move the Fm shape (6th string root) to the 3rd fret it becomes Gm. Furthermore, if you raise it from there one fret, it becomes G♯m; lowered one fret it becomes G♭m.

6th String Root

F	Fm	F7	Fm7

6th String Root		5th String Root	
0	E	0	A
1	F	2	B
3	G	↑	3	C
5	A	♭	5	D
7	B		7	E
8	C	♯	8	F
10	D	↓	10	G
12	E		12	A

5th String Root

B♭	B♭m	B♭7	B♭m7

Concise Dictionary of Musical Terms

While this brief glossary will give you basic definitions for terms used in this book and elsewhere, I recommend purchasing a music dictionary at some point in your musical studies.

A tempo – return to original tempo

Accelerando (accel.) – gradually faster

Accidental – sharps, flats, or naturals occurring apart from the key signature

Adagio – *at ease*, slower than andante

Allegretto – moderately fast

Allegro – quickly

Andante – gracefully, a walking tempo

Andantino – slightly faster than andante

Anular (*a*) – right-hand ring finger

Arpeggio – broken chord

Bar line – vertical line dividing measures on the staff

Bar (barre) – to depress two or more strings simultaneously with the index finger

Bass – low notes

Cadence – musical resolution of harmony at end of piece or section

Chord – three or more notes heard simultaneously

Chromatic – proceeding by half-steps; non-diatonic

Circle of 5ths – the succession of keys by 5ths

Clef (𝄞) – the sign used at the beginning of the staff to determine the name of each note. Guitar music is written in the Treble (or G) clef, but sounds one octave lower than written.

Coda – ending (*lit.* tail)

Common time (𝄴) – 4/4 meter

Crescendo (◁————) – gradually louder

Cut Time (𝄵) – 2/2 meter

D.C. al Coda – return to the beginning, play to the ⊕ and skip to the *Coda*.

D.C. al Fine – return to the beginning and play to the *Fine*.

D.S. al Coda – return to the ℅, play to the ⊕ and skip to the *Coda*.

D.S. al Fine – return to the ℅ and play to the *Fine*.

Decrescendo (————▷) – gradually softer

Diatonic – of the natural scale; major or minor scale

Diminuendo – gradually softer

Dolce – *sweet* and warm, played over the soundhole

Dot – increases the value of a note by half its original value

Double bar – signifies the end of a section or piece

Double flat (♭♭) – to flat a note twice (whole-step)

Double sharp (𝄪) – to sharp a note twice

Dynamics – degrees of volume

Enharmonic – written differently but sounding the same

Etude (French) – study or exercise (*Estudio* in Spanish)

Fermata (⌢) – hold sign; hold a note longer than its original value

Fine – end

Flat (♭) – to lower a note one half-step

Form – the overall structure of a piece; also refers to the type of composition such as a fugue or minuet

Forte (*f*) – loud

Fortissimo (*ff*) – very loud

Free stroke (tirando) – to avoid resting against an adjacent string after playing a note (right hand)

Glissando – slide (also called *portamento*)

Golpe – to knock on the face of the guitar

Grace note – ornamental note

Grave – solemn

Guide finger – a finger that stays on the string while shifting to a new position

Half-step – one fret; smallest interval in music

Harmonic – bell-like tone produced by lightly touching the string (see Volume Two)

Indice (*i*) – right-hand index finger

Interval – the distance between two notes

Intonation – accuracy of pitch; playing in tune

Key – the tonality of a piece with regard to a major or minor scale

Key signature – sharps or flats at the beginning of a piece showing the key

Larghetto – a little faster than largo

Largo – slow and stately

Legato – smoothly

Leggiero – lightly, swiftly

Lento – slow

Maestoso – majestic

Major – *greater*, used in respect to key, scales, chords, or intervals (see p. 66)

Measure – the space between two bar lines

Media (*m*) – right-hand middle finger

Melody – the tune or leading part of a piece

Meter – the pulse or feel of the rhythm

Metronome – device used to keep time and indicate tempo

Mezzo-forte (*mf*) – moderately loud

Mezzo-piano (*mp*) – moderately soft

Minor – *lesser*, used in respect to key, scales, chords, or intervals (see p. 66)

Moderato – moderately

Modulation – change of key

Natural (♮) – cancels previous sharp or flat

Octave – interval of eight notes

Pedal tone – a consistent note around which other voices move

Pianissimo (*pp*) – very soft

Piano (*p*) – soft

Pitch – the highness or lowness of a note

Pivot finger – a finger that stays in place on the string as an anchor while others move around it

Pizzicato (pizz.) – muted or muffled

Planting – placing right-hand fingers on the strings in preparation to play them

Ponticello – metallic, played near the bridge

Pulgar (*p*) – right-hand thumb

Presto – very quickly

Rallentando (rall.) – gradually slower

Rasgueado – strum with fingers (Flamenco style)

Repeat sign – signifies restatement of a passage

Rest stroke (apoyando) – to bring a right-hand finger or thumb to rest against an adjacent string after playing a note

Ritardando (rit.) – gradually slower

Rolling – arpeggiating a chord

Rubato – freely slowing down or speeding up

Scale – *ladder*, step-wise succession of notes

Sforzando (*sfz*) – strong accent

Simile – continue in a similar manner

Sharp (♯) – to raise a note one half-step

Slur – hammer-on or pull-off (see Volume Two)

Staccato – *detached*, short notes

Staff – fives lines and four spaces on which music is written

Tambora – percussive effect of drumming on the strings near the bridge

Tempo – *time*, the speed of the music

Tie – a curved line joining two notes of identical pitch indicating that the first note is to be held for the value of both

Time signature – the numbers at the beginning of a piece indicating the count and meter

Tone – timbre, quality of sound

Treble – high notes

Tremolo – rapid repetition of same note

Trill – rapid alternation of two consecutive notes

Triplet – three notes played in the space of two similar ones

Unison – two notes of identical pitch

Vibrato – slight fluctuation of pitch

Vivace – lively

Voice – a musical line or part

Whole-step – two half-steps (two frets)

Fingerboard Chart

A Personal Note From Christopher Parkening...

I have a commitment to personal excellence which at its heart seeks to honor and glorify the Lord with my life and the music that I play. People often ask how my faith affects my music and my career as a concert guitarist. As a Christian, I find it helpful to contemplate verses from the Bible before and even during a performance. One of my favorites is PHILIPPIANS 4:6–7: *"Be anxious for nothing; but in everything by prayer and supplication with thanksgiving let your requests be made known unto God. And the peace of God, which passeth all understanding, shall keep your hearts and minds through Christ Jesus."* It is interesting to note that it does not say God will answer every request in the way you would expect. It does say that by trusting in Him with thanksgiving, you will have the peace to handle whatever circumstance or situation that occurs. In other words, you place the burden of responsibility upon the Lord, trusting that His will would be done. That is what gives you the peace.

Here are some other helpful verses:

ROMANS 8:28 *And we know that all things work together for good to them that love God, to them who are the called according to his purpose.*

PHILIPPIANS 4:8–9 *Finally, brethren, whatsoever things are true, whatsoever things are honest, whatsoever things are just, whatsoever things are pure, whatsoever things are lovely, whatsoever things are of good report; if there be any virtue, and if there be any praise, think on these things. Those things, which ye have both learned, and received, and heard, and seen in me, do: and the God of peace shall be with you.*

II CORINTHIANS 12:9 *And he said unto me, My grace is sufficient for thee: for my strength is made perfect in weakness. Most gladly therefore will I rather glory in my infirmities, that the power of Christ may rest upon me.*

ISAIAH 26:3 *Thou wilt keep him in perfect peace, whose mind is stayed on thee: because he trusteth in thee.*

PROVERBS 3:5–6 *Trust in the LORD with all thine heart; and lean not unto thine own understanding. In all thy ways acknowledge him, and he shall direct thy paths.*

I PETER 5:5b–7 *...be clothed with humility: for God resisteth the proud, and giveth grace to the humble. Humble yourselves therefore under the mighty hand of God, that he may exalt you in due time: casting all your care upon him; for he careth for you.*

ISAIAH 12:2 *Behold, God is my salvation: I will trust, and not be afraid.*

JOHN 3:16 *For God so loved the world, that he gave his only begotten Son, that whosoever believeth in him should not perish, but have everlasting life.*

Most people believe you need to be confident in order to play a good concert. I understand, however, that God does not want us to take confidence in our own ability, and I realize that I am inadequate for the task ahead. This requires me to depend totally on God's power and grace to sustain me. Likewise then, it is a source of peace and comfort to look back and remember God's grace in past performances and trust that His grace will be sufficient for this one as well. Backstage, I constantly remind myself of what I know to be true. For example, *"All things work together for good..."*

Personally, I ultimately desire to please the Lord with my music. I dedicate every performance to my Lord and Savior Jesus Christ and consequently, the "approval" of the audience is secondary. For more insight on this topic, I recommend reading *Anxiety Attacked* by John MacArthur, Jr. (Victor Books).

Many people have asked me how to become an excellent guitarist. I answer, "Be a hard-working perfectionist," which personally makes up for my lack of talent in a lot of areas. Our goal should be to overcome what we lack in talent or ability by what we have in dedication and commitment. This takes self-discipline—the ability to regulate your conduct by principles and sound judgment, rather than by impulse, desire, high pressure, or social custom. It is the ability to subordinate the body to what is right and what is best. Self-discipline means nothing more than to order the priorities of your life. It is the bridge between thought and accomplishment, the glue that binds inspiration to achievement. For me, as a Christian, self-discipline is first of all to obey the word of God—the Bible. It is to bring my desires, my emotions, my feelings, and all that is in my life under the control of God supremely, so that I may live an obedient life which has as its goal the glory of God.

The aim and final reason of all music should be none else but the glory of God.

—Johann Sebastian Bach

CHRISTOPHER PARKENING ranks as one of the world's preeminent virtuosos of the classical guitar. His concerts and recordings consistently receive the highest worldwide acclaim. *The Washington Post* cited "his stature as the leading guitar virtuoso of our day, combining profound musical insight with complete technical mastery of his instrument." Parkening is the recognized heir to the legacy of the great Spanish guitarist Andrés Segovia, who proclaimed that "Christopher Parkening is a great artist — he is one of the most brilliant guitarists in the world."

Parkening's rare combination of dramatic virtuosity and eloquent musicianship has captivated audiences from New York to Tokyo. He has performed at the White House, appeared with Placido Domingo on *Live from Lincoln Center,* participated in Carnegie Hall's 100th Anniversary celebration, and performed twice on the internationally televised Grammy® Awards.

Parkening has appeared on many nationally broadcast television programs including *The Tonight Show, Good Morning America, 20/20, CBS Sunday Morning,* and *The Today Show.* Parkening was also featured soloist with composer/conductor John Williams on the soundtrack for the Columbia Pictures film, *Stepmom.* Having been voted "Best Classical Guitarist" in a nationwide reader's poll of *Guitar Player* magazine for many years running, he was placed in their *Gallery of the Greats* along with Andrés Segovia, John Williams, and Julian Bream.

Parkening has amassed a prolific discography on Angel records and EMI Classics. He is the recipient of two Grammy® nominations in the category of Best Classical Recording for *Parkening and the Guitar* and *The Pleasures of Their Company* (a collaboration with soprano Kathleen Battle). In celebration of Parkening's 25th year as a best-selling EMI artist, a collection of his most popular recordings entitled *Christopher Parkening – The Great Recordings* was released. EMI also released his critically acclaimed recording of Joaquín Rodrigo's *Concierto de Aranjuez* and *Fantasia para un gentilhombre,* together with the world premiere of William Walton's *Five Bagatelles for Guitar and Orchestra.* Rodrigo himself was present for the recording, which he called "magnificent."

Other important recording releases include *A Tribute to Segovia* (dedicated to the great Spanish guitarist and recorded on one of the Maestro's own concert guitars) and *Parkening Plays Vivaldi* with the Academy of St. Martin in the Fields featuring favorite concertos plus the world premiere recording of Peter Warlock's *Capriol (Suite for Guitar and String Orchestra).* Parkening also collaborated with Julie Andrews in *The Sounds of Christmas* with the London Symphony Orchestra on the Hallmark label, which sold over a million copies in its first year of release. Sony Classical also released his Christmas album with Kathleen Battle entitled *Angel's Glory.*

Parkening's commitment to his instrument extends beyond his demanding performance and recording schedule. Each summer, he teaches a master class at Montana State University in Bozeman, Montana. He has authored *The Christopher Parkening Guitar Method, Volume II* (the companion to this volume), as well as

numerous folios of guitar transcriptions and arrangements which he has recorded, all published by Hal Leonard Corporation.

Parkening has received commendations throughout his career honoring his dedication and artistry, including an honorary Doctorate of Music from Montana State University and the Outstanding Alumnus Award from the University of Southern California "in recognition of his outstanding international achievement and in tribute to his stature throughout the world as America's preeminent virtuoso of the classical guitar."

Christopher and his wife Theresa reside in Southern California. He is a world class fly-fishing and casting champion who has won the International Gold Cup Tarpon Tournament (the Wimbledon of fly-fishing) held in Islamorada, Florida.

JACK MARSHALL (1921-1973) was born in El Dorado, Kansas. He began playing the ukulele when he was ten, and graduated to jazz guitar in his early teens by listening to the recordings of Django Reinhardt. His family moved to Hollywood in the early 1930's, where he eventually became the staff guitarist for the MGM studio orchestra. He developed into a composer and conductor in the early 1950's, becoming musical director at Capitol Records. Marshall introduced the guitar as a background to film music, creating scores for several movies and television series, including *Thunder Road* and *The Munsters.*

However, his first love was the classical guitar and his favorite guitarist, Andrés Segovia. Jack Marshall served as the inspiration and mentor for his cousin, Christopher Parkening, and, as one of the few composers who understood writing for the guitar, his arrangements continue to be popular with guitarists worldwide.

DAVID BRANDON has made numerous concert and television appearances throughout North America, Europe, and Asia. The *Los Angeles Times* has called him "an outstanding technician whose precise control of details is stunning to experience." He has toured extensively with Christopher Parkening and performed with him on *Virtuoso Duets,* released by Angel/EMI. Brandon also appeared with Parkening on the Julie Andrews Hallmark Christmas album.

Brandon began playing guitar at age eight with instruction from his father. At thirteen, he attended master classes under Michael Lorimer as the youngest member of the class. After a year of study and performances in Spain and England, Brandon returned to the United States to study with Christopher Parkening on scholarship at Montana State University. He later studied with Andrés Segovia at the University of Southern California in his 1981 Master Class.

Brandon regularly gives master classes and lectures at colleges and universities across the nation. He has been the guitar advisor for the National Federation of Music Clubs and a judge for the Music Teachers National Association. David lives with his wife Sharee' and two sons in Lubbock, Texas, where he operates a private guitar studio.

The Christopher Parkening Discography

In the Spanish Style CDC-7-47194-2

Parkening Plays Bach CDC-7-47191-2

Simple Gifts CDC-7-47525-2

A Bach Celebration CDC-7-47195-2

Pleasures of Their Company CDC-7-47196-2

Virtuoso Duets CDC-7-49406-2

A Tribute to Segovia CDC-7-49404-2

Joaquin Rodrigo and William Walton Concertos CDC-7-54665-2

The Artistry of Christopher Parkening CDC-7-54853-2-5

Christopher Parkening – The Great Recordings ZDCB-54905-2-7

Parkening Plays Vivaldi CDC-5-55052-2

*Angels' Glory SK 62723

*Stepmom SK 61649

Christopher Parkening Celebrates Segovia CDC-7243-5-56730-0-8

*All albums distributed by EMI/Angel Records except *Angels' Glory*
and *Stepmom* distributed by Sony Classical.

THE PUBLICATIONS OF
CHRISTOPHER PARKENING

CHRISTOPHER PARKENING – DUETS AND CONCERTOS

Throughout his career, Christopher Parkening has had the opportunity to perform with many of the world's leading artists and orchestras, and this folio contains many selections from those collaborations. All of the pieces included here have been edited and fingered for the guitar by Christopher Parkening himself.
00690938...$24.99

THE CHRISTOPHER PARKENING GUITAR METHOD, VOL. 1 – REVISED

in collaboration with
Jack Marshall and David Brandon
Learn the art of the classical guitar with this premier method for beginners by one of the world's preeminent virtuosos and the recognized heir to the legacy of Andrés Segovia. Learn basic classical guitar technique by playing beautiful pieces of music, including over 50 classical pieces, 26 exercises, and 14 duets. Includes notes in the first position, how to hold the guitar, tuning, right and left hand technique, arpeggios, tone production, placement of fingers and nails, flats, naturals, key signatures, the bar, and more. Also includes many helpful photos and illustrations, plus sections on the history of the classical guitar, selecting a guitar, guitar care, and more.
00695228 Book..$12.99
00696023 Book/Online Audio $19.99

THE CHRISTOPHER PARKENING GUITAR METHOD, VOL. 2

Intermediate to Upper-Intermediate Level
Continues where Vol. 1 leaves off. Teaches: all notes in the upper position; tone production; advanced techniques such as tremolo, harmonics, vibrato, pizzicato and slurs; practice tips; stylistic interpretation; and more. The first half of the book deals primarily with technique, while the second half of the book applies the technique with repertoire pieces. As a special bonus, this book includes 32 previously unpublished Parkening edition pieces by composers including Dowland, Bach, Scarlatti, Sor, Tarrega and other, plus three duets for two guitars.
00695229 Book..$12.99
00696024 Book/Online Audio $19.99

PARKENING AND THE GUITAR – VOL. 1

Music of Two Centuries:
Popular New Transcriptions for Guitar
Virtuoso Music for Guitar
Ten transcriptions for solo guitar of beautiful music from many periods and styles, edited and fingered by Christopher Parkening. All pieces are suitable for performance by the advanced guitarist. Ten selections: Afro-Cuban Lullaby • Empress of the Pagodes (Ravel) • Menuet (Ravel) • Minuet in D (Handel) • Passacaille (Weiss) • Pastourelle (Poulenc) • Pavane for a Dead Princess (Ravel) • Pavane for a Sleeping Beauty (Ravel) • Preambulo (Scarlatti-Ponce) • Sarabande (Handel).
00699105...$9.95

PARKENING AND THE GUITAR – VOL. 2

Music of Two Centuries:
Popular New Transcriptions for Guitar
Virtuoso Music for Guitar
Nine more selections for the advanced guitarist: Clair de Lune (Debussy) • Giga (Visée) • The Girl with the Flaxen Hair (Debussy) • Gymnopedie Nos. I-III (Satie) • The Little Shepherd (Debussy) • The Mysterious Barricades (Couperin) • Sarabande (Debussy).
00699106...$9.95

CHRISTOPHER PARKENING – ROMANZA

Virtuoso Music for Guitar
Three wonderful transcriptions edited and fingered by Parkening: Catalonian Song • Rumores de la Caleta • Romance.
00699103...$9.99

CHRISTOPHER PARKENING – SACRED MUSIC FOR THE GUITAR, VOL. 1

Seven inspirational arrangements, transcriptions and compositions covering traditional Christian melodies from several centuries. These selections appear on the Parkening album Sacred Music for the Guitar. Includes: Präludium (Bach) • Our Great Savior • God of Grace and God of Glory (2 guitars) • Brethren, We Have Met to Worship • Deep River • Jesus, We Want to Meet • Evening Prayer.
00699095...$12.99

CHRISTOPHER PARKENING – SACRED MUSIC FOR THE GUITAR, VOL. 2

Seven more selections from the album *Sacred Music for the Guitar:* Hymn of Christian Joy (guitar and harpsichord) • Simple Gifts • Fairest Lord Jesus • Stir Thy Church, O God Our Father • All Creatures of Our God and King • Glorious Things of Thee Are Spoken • Praise Ye the Lord (2 guitars).
00699100...$12.99

CHRISTOPHER PARKENING – SOLO PIECES

Sixteen transcriptions for solo guitar edited and fingered by Parkening, including: Allegro • Danza • Fugue • Galliard • I Stand at the Threshold • Prelude • Sonata in D • Suite Española • Suite in D Minor • and more.
00690939...$19.99

PARKENING PLAYS BACH

Virtuoso Music for Guitar
Nine transcriptions edited and fingered by Parkening: Preludes I, VI & IX • Gavottes I & II • Jesu, Joy of Man's Desiring • Sheep May Safely Graze • Wachet Auf, Ruft Uns Die Stemme • Be Thou with Me • Sleepers Awake (2 guitars).
00699104...$9.95

CHRISTOPHER PARKENING – VIRTUOSO PERFORMANCES

This DVD features performances and career highlights from classical guitar virtuoso Christopher Parkening (filmed in 1971, 1973, 1998 and 2003). Viewers can watch feature titles in their entirety or select individual songs. As a bonus, there is archival footage of Andrés Segovia performing in studio, circa 1950. The DVD also includes an informational booklet. 95 minutes.
00320506 DVD $24.99

HAL•LEONARD®

www.halleonard.com

Prices, contents and availability subject to change without notice.